My Angel Walks With Me

Mona Barnes

with

LaurieAnne Blanchard

All scripture quotations unless otherwise noted are from *The Holy Bible*, King James
Version. New York: American Bible Society: 1999; Bartleby.com, 2000.

ISBN: 0692596100
ISBN-13: 978-0692596104

*This book is dedicated to the love of my life,
my husband, Jack, who has had to read these stories
for over 54 years, and without whom this book would
never have been written.*

*I would also like to dedicate this book to my beloved
children, grandchildren, great-grandchildren, and
great-great-grandchildren.*

CONTENTS

ACKNOWLEDGMENTS

No book is ever written without a team, and this book is no different. It would not be your hands without the help and work of the following people:

My daughter Laurie, who wrung these stories, one at a time, out of me. We spent hours reliving my and your past. I miss those extra hours we spent together.

A very special thanks to our family editor, Aaron, for his encouragement and hard work. No editor has had to go the extra mile like he has with this project. This book arrived at his door printed out in hard copy with stick-it notes attached to each chapter. He converted this pile of almost random paper into the manuscript you see today.

Finally, a thank you to Ravastra Design Studio for their beautiful cover art. It has made the book look the way I had hoped it would.

The Lord has blessed me with the hard work and help of these people.

PROLOGUE

WHEN I WAS SIX YEARS OLD and a very terrified little girl, Jesus heard and answered my prayer. He has performed miracles and answered prayers in my life ever since. I have never doubted that he loves me.

My family members, friends and strangers have seen these evidences of divine intervention take place. One day a young man telephoned me and pleaded with me to come tell these stories to his church. His minister would not be able to make it, and they had no one else to take the eleven o'clock hour. At first I refused, but after prayer, accepted.

Soon other ministers were asking me to tell my miracle stories to "their" congregations. Later my church's conference gave me a musical singing group for accompaniment called *His Reflections*, and paid us to travel to the churches in our conference in Oregon and Washington.

When I moved to California, I was invited to speak in our churches in the Sacramento area and in our conference church in Sunnyvale, and as well as in Nevada.

In a strange accident, when I was in my sixties, I received a brain injury, which took away my self-confidence. Terrifying flashbacks caused me to think I was in my mid-thirties. I did not recognize my husband (he had aged!) or my youngest two children, who were born late in life. This made me afraid to get up and speak in public, to represent Christ and his love for us. I became afraid I might say one thing, and mean another. However, God can work with the most humble of messengers. With his strength, I have become more confident, and wish once more to share my true experiences of hope, and faith.

I was asked by my church to compile these miracle stories for publication in a book. My husband, my children and my church feel the time has come to put these incidents down on paper as an encouragement to others to help them realize the depth of God's love.

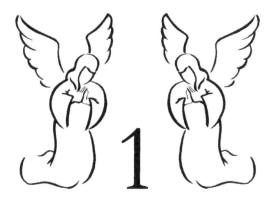

THE BELOVED FACE OF JESUS

WHEN WE MOVED TO SAN FRANCISCO, we lived in a large, two-story home. It was traumatic for me sleeping upstairs away from the sound of mother's voice, in a room all by myself.

I was only six. My four brothers all slept in the largest upstairs bedroom, and they kept their door shut. There was a long dark hallway between their bedroom and mine.

At the bottom of the stairs was the front room. This door was always kept closed because we saved it for special company; down the hall there was another door kept shut, which led into the kitchen and another door beyond that, which led into the family room, where Mom and Dad spent evenings by the fireplace.

I would use any excuse I could think of to go downstairs; it was a comforting feeling to just look at them. My father would be working his crossword puzzle, and Mom would be rocking and darning socks. They usually had the small Silvertone radio playing music sponsored by the Firestone Company. Mom would take me on her lap, and rock me for a few minutes. Later, Dad would quietly say, "Mona, it is time to go back to bed; your mother is tired."

After Mom gave me another kiss, I went back to bed. It was a long, dark walk from the safety of my mother's arms.

At the top of the stairs was a screw-in light bulb. If the light wasn't already on, I walked with my fingers brushing the walls until I reached my bedroom door. I hit my nose on the closed door a couple of times, expecting it to be open. I learned by standing on my tiptoes, I could reach the light and screw in the bulb.

My brothers' mischievous streaks added to my fears. Mom would tell the boys, "Leave the light on so Mona can see how to get to bed," but Elton's and Henry's biggest fun seemed to be to remove the light bulb and wait quietly for me to come back upstairs and try to screw it in. With the light switch permanently on, my finger often would slide into an empty socket. I jumped up and down, screaming from the shock, and I could hear my brothers chortling with glee. With the doors shut, Mom could not hear my screaming. I never told my parents what the boys were doing because that would be tattling. I had learned early on, if I wanted to play with my brothers, I couldn't tattle.

Being lonely, I visited my brothers' bedroom at night. I lay at the foot of their beds, and while I huddled under the blanket, my brothers liked to tell me scary stories. Later, after I traversed the dark path back to my room, I would imagine all kinds of horrible things.

One day, while sitting on the sidewalk and playing jacks, I noticed a man come out of the house across the street from us. The owners were at work, and I thought it was strange I didn't know this man. He seemed to be in a hurry. I stopped playing and watched him as he came down the long stairs of their home, then turned and rushed down the street.

After the Harringtons came home from work, Mrs. Harrington knocked on our door and asked if any of us had seen anybody at her home. She was asking all the neighbors.

Mom said, "No, I keep busy cleaning and cooking and the way my home is situated, I never see anybody in the street unless I come to the front of the house."

Speaking up, I commented, "I saw a man come out of your home this morning."

Her head swiveled towards me. "What did you say?"

"I saw a man come out of your house while I was playing jacks."

"Mrs. West, do you mind if the police speak to Mona? They will be here in a few moments. I have filed a police report, so the insurance company will reimburse me for the things stolen."

"Of course not, if you think it will help."

"Mona, would you tell the police what you saw?"

I nodded my head. I thought about the police and decided I didn't have to be afraid of talking to them as Daddy told me they were my best friends.

When the two policemen came, they asked me a lot of questions. One of them lowered himself and knelt down to talk to me on my level, which made it easier since I didn't have to lift my head up so high.

"Have you ever seen this man before?" he asked.

"No."

"Did you get a good look at him?"

"I watched him until he was out of sight."

"Why did you do that?"

"Cause he didn't belong here."

They looked amused and one policeman commented, "Good intuition."

"Can you tell us how tall he was?"

I looked the two men over, and decided he was just a little taller than the one standing. When I told them this, they looked at each other, and then one of them commented, "Over six feet tall."

"Was he fat or skinny?"

Again I looked at them and said he looked about like they did.

"Average build."

"Mona, can you tell us what kind of clothes he was wearing?"

"He had church pants."

They smiled at each other and commented, "Suit pants."

"What about his coat? Was it a church coat?"

"No, it was a coat that came down to his knees."

Again a smile, and the older policeman said, "An overcoat."

"Can you tell us what his hair or face looked like?"

I thought for a few minutes, and then said, "He has black hair and a mustache."

Mrs. Harrington groaned. The police turned to her, and asked her, "Does this description fit anyone you know?"

She looked sick, and nodded her head.

The policeman stood up, and turning to me said, "Honey, you have done a very good job in helping the police solve a crime. You can go back and play now. Mrs. Harrington, let's go to your house and discuss this."

I never found out any more about the crime. No one talked about it in my presence, but it worried me, knowing a crime had been committed across the street from our house.

Later one day, I was coloring in my color book, when there was a knock at the door, and when Mom and I answered the door, I heard the lady say, "Mrs. West, you are new on the block, but I have to talk to someone. My name is Mrs. Safley."

"Come in, and I'll fix a cup of coffee for you."

"Oh, that would be wonderful."

I went back to my color book. My brothers were outside playing and didn't want me to join them.

Mrs. Safley said, "The most terrible thing has happened and I am so upset."

"What is that?"

"Do you know Mrs. Wood?"

"No, I don't. Why?"

"She lives in the yellow house in the next block. Mr. and Mrs. Wood went out for dinner, and when they came home they found their fourteen-year-old daughter had been molested. She was hysterical and they had to take her to the hospital. Now I am so worried about my daughters."

"Oh, how terrible."

Totally forgetting I could hear them, they continued talking in worried tones. I stopped coloring and wondered what molest meant, but I knew from the shocked tones of voices, it wasn't good.

My bedroom window looked out over the top of the neighbor's attached, flat roofed house, which then overlooked the next neighbor's house. Deciding to see if a molester or robber could get in our house, I climbed out my bedroom window and walked across the neighbor's roof and looked down the slightly terraced roofs of the next houses. It didn't take me long to realize anyone who wanted to climb to the roof of the bottom house, could quickly climb across the other roofs until they were at my window. It was only about a three foot drop to each house. Being six years old, with an active imagination, I became a fearful little girl.

When night arrived and it was time for sleep, I lay awake shaking, and imagined every robber in town was about to climb through my bedroom window. The boys were quiet, having fallen asleep.

I called and called Mom, but my parents couldn't hear me through all the doors and hallways. Taking my blanket, I walked down to my brothers' bedroom, opened the door, and tiptoed into their room. I climbed up on the foot of my brothers' bed for security. Sighing deeply, I pulled out their covers and slipped into the foot of their bed. I lay down to go to sleep. Just as I started to drift off, my brother Henry kicked me. I shifted my body, and soon Elton's foot connected. Again I tried to shift out of their way. It was too late. Elton raised up his head to see why he couldn't stretch out, and saw me at the foot of their bed.

Elton roared, "What the heck are you doing in my bed?"

"I am afraid, and I want company."

In a sleepy voice, he said, "Go get in your own bed—there's no room for you here."

Climbing out, I looked over at Billy's bed. It looked as if there would be more room there, as he was smaller. Slipping into the foot of his bed, he was soon irritated with me, when he found out he couldn't stretch because someone was occupying the foot of his bed.

He ordered me to go back to my own room.

Back down the long, dark hall I trudged, dragging my little blanket with me. After climbing into my bed, I again tried to sleep. It was impossible. Terror had taken over my life. Finally, in my fear, I started praying, "Now I lay me down to sleep. I pray the Lord my soul to keep. In the morning when I wake, guide my steps for Jesus' sake." I repeated this over and over. I didn't know any other way to pray.

Soon I noticed that a soft light seemed to be glowing in my bedroom, and on my bedroom wall I saw the softly illuminated face of Jesus, whom I recognized from my book of memory verses. I relaxed and stared at his beautiful, loving face until I fell asleep. His softly lit face appeared every night, bringing me peace and comfort.

Eventually, when I became able to go to sleep alone in the dark, His face no longer appeared. However, I still felt as if Jesus was cradling me in his arms, and I knew His comforting presence completely surrounded me. I was finally able to fail asleep, feeling safe and loved.

"Trust in the Lord, and do good; so shalt thou dwell in the land, and verily thou shalt be fed."
Psalm 37:3

THE MAN IN WHITE

AFTER MOVING TO SAN FRANCISCO, my father only worked part time. Often, we wondered where our next meal was coming from. Then Dad, Mom, as well as all of us, came down with the flu. Dad's developed into pneumonia.

We did not know our neighbors. We did not have a telephone, so with no money, and no telephone, it was difficult to get medical help.

My bed was in a little alcove off my parent's bedroom. I could see them from where I slept. While lying in my bed, I could hear my heart pounding loudly in my ears. This had never happened to me before, and I wondered what was wrong. My head throbbed, and I kept drifting in and out of sleep.

I knew my parents were also sick, because they never came near my bed. They just laid there sleeping, too sick to get up. They didn't seem to wake up at all. I worried they were going to die, and wondered if I would, also.

When I awoke I was very thirsty, but was too weak to get out of bed and go get anything to drink. I assumed my brothers were sick also, as they never came in our bedroom to see us.

When my thirst became unbearable, I heard the soft whisper of footsteps enter my bedroom. A young man appeared. He wore white clothes and white, soft-soled shoes. He looked about thirty years old, and had a pleasant face. As he neared my bed, I watched him come and bend over me. I lifted my heavy eyes to look up at him and he smiled reassuringly. He helped me sit up, and held me as he raised a glass of water to my lips. After I had drunk my fill, he laid me gently back in bed. He gave me a cold sponge bath and then, before he left, he put a cold cloth on my forehead. This felt so good to my aching head.

I wondered why he never went near my parents, but he always quietly left the room after tending to me. Each time I aroused, I could hear his soft footsteps come near, and again, he would hold me up and help me drink water. He straightened my bed sheets so I would be more comfortable. I assumed when he left me, he went to take care of my brothers, but they didn't remember seeing him.

This man in white silently took care of me. I never questioned his sudden appearance, or where he came from when I needed him the most. He simply appeared without speaking a word.

My stranger took care of me while Mom and Dad were too sick to do it. He never spoke to me, but I always felt comforted by his presence. After Mom improved and could take care of me herself, I never saw this man dressed in white again.

Was he my guardian angel?

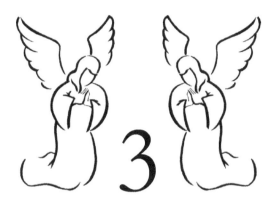

THE STEVEDORE

MY FATHER BELIEVED IN GOD, but was not a practicing Christian. He always backed Mom up in what she believed, but never attended church with us. When we had worship at night, Mom did the praying.

As a young man in his late thirties, it must have been very stressful to be the sole provider for eight people. When the depression hit, Dad lost his job, our home in Stockton, his brand-new car, and the investment property he owned in downtown Oakland, CA. His stock became worthless. Things kept getting worse as time went by. When we lost everything, we moved to San Francisco, where he obtained work at Ray Oil Burner.

As the work was cut back at Ray Oil Burner, out of loyalty to his crew, the foreman refused to lay off any of his men. He kept hoping things would get better, so the owner just kept cutting back everyone's working hours. This allowed the men to work every other week, but it wasn't enough for anyone to live on. Unemployment benefits and welfare had not yet been created by our government. When the day finally came that Dad worked only a few days once a month, he knew we were in serious trouble.

He found a part time job passing out advertisements for a cleaning business. He left early in the morning, and placed the postcards at each door. This didn't pay very much, but it brought a little food into the home. Dad painted the houses our landlord owned, and this paid for our rent, assuring a roof over our heads.

When he had painted all the houses the landlord owned, Dad looked for other work. He left each day, looking for work of any kind, to supplement his diminishing income. Each night when he came home, he looked a little wearier, a little more desperate. Mom looked at him, and he would quietly shake his head, "No."

Mom continued with her prayers.

Every day we ran to greet him when he came up our hill in San Francisco. We shouted, "Daddy's home, Daddy's home." We clung to his weary arms, telling him how we missed him. We had no idea how exhausted and weary he felt. Not realizing the seriousness of the situation, we looked forward to his playing games with us. We did know the helpings on our plate seemed to get smaller, and often complained about just eating beans and potatoes. While Dad looked grim and unhappy, Mom spent more time on her knees, praying to her heavenly Father.

The day finally came when Mom told Dad, "Fay, there is very little food left in the house."

Dad sighed, and quietly said, "Maybe you'd better pray for some money or food."

This surprised me, as I had never heard Dad pray. He joined us in saying the Lord's Prayer, but this was the only time I ever heard him pray out loud. Each night during family worship, Mom knelt and prayed for help to feed her family. When we got up from praying, I looked at my father and he always wore a peculiar look on his face I could not interpret.

One evening he asked Mom, "Emily, do you really think this is going to help? You've been praying for a long time, and your prayers haven't been answered."

"God will take care of us," my mother replied confidently.

Dad shook his head. "Do you really think God is going to take time out just to take care of our little affairs?"

Mom smiled, "He's not going to let my children go hungry."

I began to worry about whether God would listen to my mother, or if my father was correct and God was too busy with the universe and world affairs to worry about whether we ate or not. Dad plainly had his doubts that God would answer Mom, and I thought my father knew everything. I hoped my mother knew God better than my father.

One evening when Dad was out of work for a whole month and the situation at home was desperate, the doorbell rang. We were all surprised, as we were not acquainted with anyone in our neighborhood. Dad went to the door. Soon he called, "Emily, come here!"

This was a sign for all of us to rush to the front door. One of our neighbors stood there. He was a tall, rugged, muscular man. He said he worked as a stevedore on the docks in San Francisco. Dad had a stunned look on his face, and he said, "This is Mr. Gurtler. Sir, do you mind telling my wife what you just told me?"

Mr. Gurtler replied, "Not at all. I noticed you have a large family, and my wife tells me she has not seen you go to work for a month. It's bothering her, and anything that bothers my wife, bothers me. I kept thinking what would I do if I didn't have an income for a month? How would I feed my children? So after discussing this, my wife and I felt we should give you my salary this payday."

He offered the money to Dad, but Dad motioned for him to give the money to Mom. He said, "She is the one who prayed for help. Give it to her."

He handed my mother a large bundle of paper money. More than I ever noticed Dad giving Mom. He went on to say, "I couldn't sleep until I decided to do this."

Mom started to cry, and thanked Mr. Gurtler over and over. She said, "Fay, there's enough here to pay our rent, our utility bills, buy groceries, and get Everett the pair of shoes he needs."

Mr. Gurtler then asked, "We have a daughter Mona's age, and we would be very pleased if she could eat supper with us each Tuesday. Would that be alright?"

Mom agreed, and each Tuesday for dinner, instead of beans and potatoes, I had a lamb chop, creamed peas with new potatoes, a delicious salad, and a mouth-watering pie.

My siblings were a little envious.

I learned that day that God is interested in our little worries and he does answer prayers.

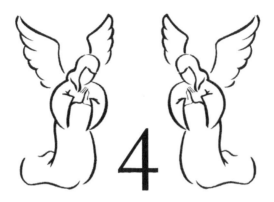

A TOUGH DECISION

THE FOG WAS THICK and dripping, shutting out all signs of life. The cold seemed to seep in through the windows and under the door. We didn't have the money to buy wood to keep the fireplace going, and the gas company was threatening to shut off our supply. Our food stores were very low. The depression of the thirties was hitting our home hard.

Dad had lost our home in Stockton because he didn't have the money to pay the taxes. We left his brand new car in the garage, because there was no money to pay for the gas to drive it. A friend moved our furnishings to what seemed an unfriendly land in San Francisco, because this was where Dad had finally found a job.

Out of each pay check, he donated to the San Francisco Community Chest fund, to help those who needed food. When the day came we needed help, he went to apply, and the authorities told him that because our home was three houses over the San Francisco/Daly City line, we did not qualify. He needed to apply to Daly City Community Fund. He came home bitter, because although he donated and worked in San Francisco, they turned him down. The next day he walked to the Daly City Community Fund, to ask for some food for his hungry family, and they turned him down also. Because he worked in San Francisco, and donated to their fund, he had fallen between the cracks. Life looked very bleak to my parents.

I overheard Mom talking quietly to Dad, and she told him she was pregnant. He asked her, "Are you sure?"

"Yes, Fay, I am sure. What are we going to do?"

I strained my ears to hear the answer, but there was just silence. Finally Dad quietly said, "Emily, I can't feed the seven children we have! How are we going to pay a doctor to deliver a baby, and how are we going to clothe a new baby, let alone feed another mouth?"

Mom began softly crying. For the next few days, depression had not only hit our country hard, but now it seemed to have settled in our home also. Mom and Dad both looked as if they had just lost a loved one. Neither one spoke more than necessary. Silence seemed to have taken over our home.

Mom loved us and made each of us feel we were her special, favorite child. I knew I was, but for some reason, my brothers thought they were too, and we all knew our oldest sister and baby brother were her favorites - maybe next to ourselves. Instead of showing joy at the prospect of another baby, sadness had taken over our home.

One day I overheard Mom confiding in her new friend, Mrs. Harrington, who lived across the street from us. Mrs. Harrington thought she had the perfect solution. "My doctor will perform the abortion, and Paul will drive you to Dr. Young's clinic."

"I don't think I could go through with an abortion. Isn't it dangerous?"

"No, Emily, I've had several, myself. You even come home the same day."

I puzzled over their conversation, and decided to consult my brother, Henry, who was ten years old. I felt Henry knew just about everything.

"Henry, Mrs. Harrington wants Mom to have an abortion. What does abortion mean?"

"I don't know, but let's look the word up in the dictionary. That's what Dad always tells us to do."

We located the dictionary, and looked up the word, and it said "the voluntary removal of a fetus in order to terminate a pregnancy before it is able to survive."

We looked at each other, and didn't like the sounds of this. So we decided to look up the word fetus and see what it meant- and it meant the "unborn young of an animal, especially a human."

This meant that, if they had not wanted us, they could have aborted us, and we would not exist. This was heavy thinking for us. We shut the dictionary, and looked at each other, and I know I felt sick. We were silent for a while, and then decided this needed some discussion. We thought about what would happen if we had a new baby, and decided we could handle having another one. Henry and I felt the baby could wear Everett's outgrown clothes. We knew Everett was sick all the time, and Mom spent a lot of time with him. He had been born with pneumonia and never seemed to really get well. How could Mom continue to give Everett the care he needed, if she had a new baby?

We decided it would be up to us to help out. We could take care of the new baby, if Everett became real sick.

We discussed all the aspects of what life would be like with or without a new baby. We could not accept the idea Mom would actually go through with an abortion. We stared at both Mom and Dad for several days, wondering what they would do. When I looked at Mrs. Harrington, it was with disillusioned eyes, knowing she chose to have abortions rather than babies. The big question was, *What would Mom decide to do?*

We never said anything to Mom or Dad about knowing what they were planning on doing, but it scared us. We couldn't help thinking they could have done what Mrs. Harrington did, and we wouldn't be here. We tried to imagine what life would be like without each other.

This was serious.

One morning, when I went into the family room, I found Mom dressed to go out. I knew the day had come, and she had decided to have an abortion. She had on her coat and hat, and was looking miserable. Her head was lying on the table, and she wouldn't lift her head or acknowledge I was near her. Feeling sick myself, I put my arms around her, to tell her I loved her. She patted my hands, and this was all the acknowledgment she showed. Realizing she would never know the comfort of this tiny baby's arms, I could hear her very quietly praying, "Oh, God, help me, help me! I can't do this terrible deed. And yet I can't afford not to do it. How will my children eat?"

Suddenly, she sat up with a smile on her face, and looked as if she had a new lease on life. This surprised me, but I felt better, just seeing my mother smile again.

Dad and Mrs. Harrington came into the house, and Dad told Mom, "Paul has his car warm, and is ready to take you to the doctor."

They were both surprised and shocked when Mom told them, "I'm not going. God has answered my prayers."

Accusations were heaped on her head: arguments were used, the children would starve, and she was depriving the rest of her children by her stubbornness in having this eighth child. Nothing changed her mind. Sweetly smiling, she told them, "An angel told me, 'Don't go through with this terrible deed. This baby has a special mission to fulfill for God, and she will be a comfort to you in your old age.' I believe God. Someway, somehow we will have enough food for all of the children."

Mrs. Harrington and Dad just stood there with a shocked look on their faces, but the happiness radiating from Mom's face was a thrill to see, and to know, she was not voluntarily getting rid of a baby. I couldn't help but wonder, "How does the angel know if it is going to be a boy or a girl? Mom said the angel told her, "She will be a comfort to you in your old age." Could angels really know this far in advance? It was going to be a long time for me to wait to find out if the angel was right.

DID THE ANGEL REALLY KNOW?

THE NEXT NINE MONTHS seemed to creep. Waiting for Mom to have her baby, I studied her tummy each day, as it seemed to continue to grow larger.

"Momma, how do you get a baby in your tummy?"

Momma didn't seem to know how to answer. I was examining my own tummy and finally asked, "Momma, does the baby come out here where my belly button is?"

She looked relieved, and said "Well, that is one way."

"Momma, how much longer before the baby comes?"

"In July, dear."

This satisfied me, and I went back outside to play.

Months later, in July, when I first opened my eyes, I couldn't imagine what woke me. Listening, I raised up on one arm to hear better, but the sound stopped. So I snuggled down further under the covers until my cold nose was just under the thick, soft quilt Mom and Dad had spent weeks making. The strange sounds started up again. Aunt Beulah had come to visit the week before, and she now slept upstairs in Mom and Dad's bed, and they had moved downstairs to Lillian's bed. There was a bustling sound I figured Aunt Beulah was making, and low muted voices talking. It all sounded so strange. The doorbell rang and I heard Dad going to the door. Someone was building up the fire. Cupboard doors opened and closed, and occasionally I could hear a soft moan.

This must have been what woke me up. I rolled on my side and leaned my head on my hand so I could hear better, but the noises didn't tell me anything. I crawled out of bed, wrapped my well-worn night-robe around myself, dragging my little blanket with me, and slipped into the boys' bedroom.

"Hey, Elton, wake up!" I whispered. Elton jerked awake with a nervous start and blinked his eyes at the light, which shone in from the open door.

"What is it?" Billy asked, without opening his eyes.

"It's only Mona," he replied. "Go back to sleep."

"Well, I would if you two would quit yakking your jaws," Billy snapped.

"Oh, stifle it, Bill. I was talking to Mona." Elton yawned, and then asked me what was wrong.

"Momma's crying. I can hear her."

"She's probably having the baby. Go back to sleep." Elton lay back down.

"Do you think it will be a girl like the angel told Mom?"

"Oh, for goodness sake, how would I know?" Elton snapped. Then seeing the hurt look on my face, he was a little gentler when he said, "It will probably just be another boy. It always is."

"But maybe it will be a girl."

"Will you shut up? A body can't get any sleep in this house!" complained Billy.

Henry was half asleep when he entered the conversation. "I'll bet it's just another boy. That's all Mom has."

I became indignant. "I'm a girl!"

"Yeah, but you were a mistake."

"I'm not either a mistake!"

Billy mumbled, "You are if you don't shut up and go back to bed, so I can sleep."

I wouldn't be put off. "I'll bet it's a girl. Momma said it would be..."

Everett entered the conversation. "What's a girl?"

"Shut up, Eb-Eb, go back to sleep," Henry groaned.

"What's a girl?" Everett insisted.

"Now look what you've done. You've woke the baby up," Henry groaned.

"I's not a baby! I's almost three."

"No, you're not. You're only two."

"I's not. I's two and a half. I's almost three. Daddy said I's not a baby anymore," Everett declared.

Elton raised his head, and said, "Mona, if you're not in bed by the time I count three, you are going to wish YOU were the baby!"

"I'm going. I'm going. But I don't see why no one else cares if Momma has a girl or a boy."

Henry spoke in hushed tones, "Mona, we want a little sister as much as you do, but there isn't anything we can do about it, and I'm sleepy. Now, please go to bed!"

Billy rose up and grinned, saying, "Let Elton count, Mona. Let's see what he does!"

"MONA," Elton roared.

"All right I'm going, I'm going." I slipped back into my bedroom, and continued to listen for sounds from downstairs. I thought about what life would be like with a baby sister, instead of just the four brothers to heckle and boss me. Listening to the unusual sounds emanating from downstairs, I tried to visualize what was going on, but my imagination wasn't much help.

Then I heard a tiny wail! The baby was born! Strong emotion gripped my soul. The baby was here. Was it a boy or girl? Once more, I slipped out of bed and into the boys' room, shaking Elton.

I whispered, "Elton, wake up! The baby is born! Please! Go find out if it is a boy or girl."

Elton was indignant. "Will you go back to bed?"

"Elton, please find out," I pleaded.

Grimly, Elton said, "Mona, once more and you'll wish Mom had never had YOU!"

"Okay!" Retreating, I went back to my lonely bedroom, and lay there praying for the new baby. Surely, it was a girl! But now panic began to fill me. I hadn't heard a cry after the first little wail. I wondered why. Always before when Momma had a baby, it would cry and cry. Silently praying the baby would live, I worked myself up to a fever pitch of worry. Praying no longer satisfied me. I had to know!

Once more I crept into the boys' bedroom, and looked at my four brothers who were sound asleep. Why was I the only one worried whether our new baby would live or not? Unable to stand the suspense any longer, I crept downstairs in my long, flannel nightgown, and down the dark hall. With stealth, I opened the door and peeked into the room, but Aunt Beulah noticed me.

"Mona, for goodness sake! Go to bed. You're not wanted down here. Now go to bed!"

Dr. Arthur looked up, and seeing the worry on my face said, "Any child concerned enough to come down those dark stairs and that long dark hallway to make sure her mother is all right, deserves to see her mother and her new baby sister."

A thrill shot through me. The angel was right! I had a baby sister who would be a comfort to my mother in her old age.

Dr. Arthur took me by the hand and led me to where Momma was lying in bed. Daddy was on the other side of the bed looking down at Momma with a kind of sweet, funny smile on his face.

Dr. Arthur said, "Emily, here is the baby's very first visitor, and she isn't even an hour old yet."

He showed me the baby, and I saw a tiny, shriveled up, purple-looking baby.

Shock coursed through me. "Why is she so dark looking?"

Dr. Arthur answered in a gentle voice, "She had a rough time, Honey, and the cord was wrapped around her neck. She almost didn't make it."

I murmured, "She looks like a little monkey."

All of Momma's maternal instincts sprung to life. With indignation she told me, "Mona! She does not! She is the most beautiful baby I have ever seen!"

How could I make Momma understand? The sound of the baby's first cry was music to my ears. This tiny, purple, wrinkled baby was beautiful to my eyes, also. I had been praying she would live for what seemed all night. The miracle of a newborn baby filled me with wonder, and love flooded through me. I thought, *This is MY baby sister. She belongs to me. God told Momma this baby had a special mission in life, and she would be a comfort to Momma in her old age. She is a very special baby. And I get to help take care of her.*

Still thrilled by the miracle of it all, I made no protest when Aunt Beulah took me by the hand and said firmly, "Now go to bed."

Going back upstairs, I thought about the tremendous news. I had to share it with someone, and the boys would never allow me to wake them up again. Going into my bedroom, I dressed in the dark, and once more slipped out and down the stairs. This time I eased open the front door, and tiptoed out onto the porch.

I looked up and down the dark, foggy street. The fog hung around the street lights, obliterating some of the light. I tried to decide who I should I tell the momentous news. Mr. Borelli always asked me each day, "Well, has the new baby arrived yet? Was the angel correct? Let me know as soon as the baby is born." So I decided he was the one I should go visit and tell this wonderful news to. I knew he had not gone to work yet, because the lights were not on in his house. I knew he would be happy to hear my exciting news.

Mr. Borelli looked a little disgruntled at first, then grinned and started asking me what the baby looked like. When I told him like a little monkey, he broke out laughing and said, "Oh, Mona, your mother is not going to appreciate that!" He grinned, "Mona, everyone wants to know if the angel knew what he was talking about. I suggest you wake everyone up and tell them the good news. They are really going to appreciate your doing this." Smiling from ear to ear, he told me, "Good night."

I thought Mr. Borelli had a wonderful idea. One by one, I rang doorbells or knocked to spread the wonderful news: that God had sent a baby girl to our house.

Starting at the top of the quiet block, I rang the doorbell at the first door. Imagine anyone sleeping on a morning like this, when a new baby had arrived? It was still dark, about 3 A.M., and I had to ring the doorbell several times before anyone came to the door.

Each neighbor greeted me in a different manner. Some were sleepy, but acted interested. Others were abrupt, "That's nice. Goodnight". Mr. Harrington looked amused and said, "I'm glad Emily is okay. Good night, Mona."

Mr. Gurtler stood patiently while I explained to him about how the angel had told Momma there would be a baby girl, and that "I guess angels know everything." He smiled down at me and gently said, "I guess the angels do know everything."

When I came to the house where my good friend, Dorothy, lived, she greeted me with, "Do you mean to say you woke us up at three in the morning to tell us you have a new baby at your house? So what else is new?" She slammed the door in my face.

I stood there for a few minutes, shaken by her ungrateful attitude, and decided not to go to the last house. They had just moved in, and I didn't know them. I walked back up the hill to my home, wondering why no one else shared the wonderful excitement I felt at the birth of a baby sent by God to our home.

THE WAYWARD SHOE

AT SCHOOL, ONE MORNING, I noticed my friend, Allene Vollmer, had two lunches.

"Why do you have two lunches, Allene?"

"One's for you. At dinner last night, I told Mama and Daddy you always brought one sandwich, and it was made with mashed beans. I asked Mama to make me a mashed bean sandwich, but Daddy told Mama from now on, she was to make two lunches and one was for you. So, can I have your bean sandwich?"

I gladly gave it to her, while I reveled in my wonderful lunch.

Allene lived two doors from me. Her father was a very busy pediatrician, and was always kind to me. He included me in many of their drives when he took his wife and two daughters with him.

It wasn't long after this that a messenger came into my schoolroom with a note for my teacher. Mrs. Baccigaluppi read it, looked at me, and said, "Mona, the principal wants to see you in his office."

All eyes turned on me, wondering what had I done. Fear ran through me as I followed the other girl back to the principal's office.

When I entered the office, the principal smiled and said, "Mona, you must have a guardian angel. Someone is paying for four quarts of milk to be delivered to your home every day, starting tomorrow morning. He made one stipulation. You must drink one quart of milk daily yourself, and the other three are for your whole family. I have a note for your mother telling her what the stipulation is. Now promise me you will drink one quart of milk daily. He feels you are too fragile."

I was happy to make the promise. When I arrived home with my note, my parents were thrilled. However, when a week went by, and I had a whole quart to myself daily, my brothers started to grumble.

"How come Mona gets a whole quart, and we have to share?"

Dad quickly nipped the rebellion, "Just be grateful Mona is your sister, or you wouldn't have any milk for breakfast! Mona is the reason we all can have milk on our cornmeal."

My brothers turned their eyes on me, and I could see the speculation in them. *If she can get milk for us, maybe she can get something else.*

Another week went by, and once more I was called into the principal's office. This time, I wasn't afraid. I had a clean conscience, so I wondered what else was in store for me.

Mr. Kearney met me with a smile, and said, "Mona, someone noticed you always walk with one shoulder higher than the other, and he has arranged for you to go to St Luke's Hospital for an evaluation. Here is the date of your appointment. He is paying for all of your medical bills, so tell your folks not to worry."

When I came home with the new note, my parents were all flustered. My walking this way had just seemed normal to them, as they had grown accustomed to it. My sister, Lillian, was home for a visit from where she worked, so she volunteered to take me to the hospital.

When we arrived, the doctor had Lillian take all my clothes off except for my shoes, socks and underwear. He took a piece of black chalk and marked the vertebrae on my back with it. I turned around when he was through, and he had a peculiar look on his face.

"Turn around, Mona. I want to show your sister your spine."

I turned back around and he told Lillian, "Do you see how her back curves? It is in the shape of an S; we are going to have our job cut out for us to straighten it."

He took us to a large room, where he gave orders to a young man, who then took me by the hand and led me over to equipment. For the next few years, I spent one day a week there, working out. There were ladders built into the wall, where I climbed, and then holding on with one hand, and one foot, I exercised the other arm and leg. We had rings where I learned to swing my body up, and brace my legs with the straps while standing on my head in the air, swinging back and forth. There were bars where I learned to swing my body over and under the bars. I developed wonderful muscles. Each month, the doctor would call me into his office and mark my spine. My Dad made bars for me, so I was encouraged to practice at home.

The third trip to the gym, the doctor called me into his office, and measured my feet. He told me one of my legs was one inch longer than the other leg, and he was measuring me for new shoes. This worried me. My sister Vesta was a baby, and fast growing out of her shoes, and so was Everett. Henry, Billy and I usually received one new pair of shoes a year. Our shoes were usually a little large when my parents bought them, so we could "grow into" them.

The doctor assured me my shoes were already paid for. When I received the new shoes, I was ecstatic. The doctor told me to look into the mirror, and I no longer stood with one shoulder higher. Turning, I beamed at him. "Thank you so very much! Now I look like the other girls."

He laughed and said, "Don't thank me. Thank the man who is paying for all of this."

"I don't know who it is."

"And that is the way he wants it!" He smiled back at me, and said, "Maybe you better just thank God."

So I did.

28

That evening, my brothers, Henry and Billy, the Safleys, Blandinis, Borellas, Gurtlers and Johnsons and myself, were all out in the street playing kick-the-can. This was a game we could all afford.

Whenever one of the parents was able to buy something in a can, they washed it out and saved it for us. This didn't happen too often, so tin cans were prized. We jumped in the middle of them until they curled around our shoes, and then wore them for stilts, as we clanked around the street. We also used the cans for our favorite game of kick-the- can.

We put one can in the middle of the street, someone was made "it" and another was nominated to kick the can. The minute it was kicked, all the children ran and hid. It was up to the person to find the hiding children, before someone else ran in and kicked the can, letting all the others "free" and able to run and hide again.

There was a twenty-foot-high jungle of a hedge, which had been allowed to grow wild. We had grown used to this huge hedge that towered over us. It was thick and dense. Our parents had warned us never to climb in it, as they considered it dangerous. It surrounded our block on three sides, but on the side we lived on, we had houses in front of it for half the block. We were playing in the area where there were no houses.

One evening when we were playing this game, I ran in to free the prisoners, yelling, "Olley olley, oxen free." I turned to kick the can but my shoe was not tied tightly enough. The shoe went flying into the air.

No one ran to hide. The children all stopped running and watched my special shoe arc up into the air. The game came to a complete standstill, as our eyes followed the flying shoe. When it landed in the hedge, we all groaned, and my friends looked at me with complete sympathy. I had a big lump in my throat and struggled not to cry, as I stood there wearing only one very expensive shoe.

Robert said, "You'll never see that shoe again."

Dorothy groaned as she said, "I'm so sorry, Mona, I'm so sorry."

Eugene looked up at the hedge and said, "No one will ever find that shoe. That would be like looking for a needle in a haystack."

Little Zella piped up with, "That's a monster of a hedge. Momma told me never to try to climb in it."

We stood around talking about my tragedy, and wondering what I would do for shoes, and how would we tell my parents. Finally, I decided I had better go and face the music, but Henry said, "Mona, stay out here. I'm going in and pray for Jesus to help me find your shoe."

Although every one of my friends believed in Jesus, I think no one had ever asked Him for anything before, in our 'gang of children.' We were all believers, and went to our own church regularly, but we had just never as a group thought to ask God to find something for us.

Since Henry had asked us not to do anything until he had prayed, we stood around in a group, talking about the terrible event which had just taken place.

Dorothy commented, "Have you noticed Henry always goes upstairs to pray by his open bedroom window?"

Eugene said, "He reminds me of Daniel in the Bible."

This made all of us think about how Daniel prayed in the Bible. I hoped God would listen to Henry the way he listened to Daniel.

We decided to sit in the middle of the street, waiting for Henry.

Henry prayed without letting Mom or Dad know he was in the house. After about 10 long minutes, which seemed like an hour, he casually came out and said, "Jesus told me He is going to show me where the shoe is."

Henry walked up the street like he knew where he was going, climbed through the barbwire fence separating us from the hedge, and soon was lost to our view. We could see the limbs occasionally move, but it was so thick, we could not see him at all. When the movement stopped, it became really quiet as we all waited with bated breath.

Soon the movement began again, and I had a lump in my throat, waiting for the verdict. Henry finally appeared at the top of the hedge with a big grin on his face. He called out, "Mona, catch!"

My shoe came flying back to me. We were all happy and excited, knowing God had answered Henry's prayer. Seeing God answer a prayer so fast made a lasting impression on me, and from then on I took all my troubles to God.

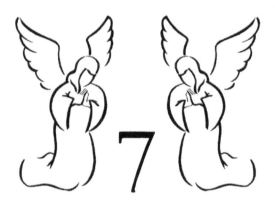

"Because thou hast made the Lord, which is my refuge, even the most High, thy habitation; there shall no evil befall thee, neither shall any plague come nigh thy dwelling."
Psalm 91:9-10

SPREAD EAGLED ON A CLIFF

ELTON AND TEX were my two big brothers. Tex wasn't a biological brother, but he adopted us, and lived with us. Sixteen-year-old Elton and seventeen-year-old Tex felt they shouldn't have to put up with me all the time. I was ten, and they were my heroes. I thought they were wonderful, and followed them everywhere. When they complained to mother that I was their shadow, she quietly said, "Then you better think of what you do and say." This wasn't the answer they wanted.

I heard Tex tell Elton, "Let's go climb the quarry."

The rock quarry near our home was like a canyon with three steep sides. The Soldiers at the Presidio used it to practice rappelling.

Thinking this was an excellent idea, I quietly put my book down, got an apple to eat, and followed them. I always wished I could see the quarry, and now was my big chance. If I was quiet, they never seemed aware when I followed them, until it was too late to send me home.

We hiked uphill a long distance, entered the canyon floor, jumped over a small creek and started climbing the sides of the cliff. I thought this was really neat, because my father told me, "The cliff is too hard for you to climb, so I don't want you going there." Thinking, *My, how easy this is to climb,* I felt a little smug, and could hardly wait to tell my father he was wrong.

When I got about half-way up the cliff, I looked down and saw the creek we had jumped over, only now it looked small. Noticing the treetops were now below where I was perching, I became frightened. Thinking I'd better hurry and climb to the top, I tried to climb a little faster, but it wasn't long until I couldn't find any places to put my hands for the next move.

Deciding I should climb back down, I ran into a new problem. I groped around, and it was impossible for me to find places to put my feet. I was spread-eagled on the face of the cliff, and I couldn't move up or down.

Looking up, I was not able to see either Tex or Elton. They had already reached the top, and disappeared from sight. I became absolutely horrified as I looked up at an empty cliff. I realized there was not another person around to help me or even knew my location. It was terrifying. I was petrified and started screaming their names, over and over, "Elton - Tex- Elton! Help! Help! Help me!"

It was several moments later before I saw Elton and Tex's face peering over the brow of the cliff. They were lying on their stomachs looking down. Their eyes were big, and their faces were both white.

Elton said, "I'm going back down after her."

Tex was more level-headed, and he said, "Elton, you can climb up without ropes, but you can't climb down without ropes because of the way the cliff is formed."

Tex continued, "I'll run around the rim of the cliff, and come back up and climb up behind her."

Elton protested, "No, I'm her brother. You talk to her and keep her calm. She'll listen to you more than to me. I'll run around and climb behind her."

Tex agreed and started talking in a soothing tone of voice, "Keep your eyes on me, Mona. Don't look down. That's my girl. Just keep your eyes on me. You know we love you and we'll keep you safe. Honey, don't look down. Mona, keep your eyes on me."

As long as I kept my eyes on Tex, I felt comparatively safe. Every time I looked down, I started sobbing again. I was shaking, and my hold was getting precarious, as I found my strength giving out. However, I managed to maintain a death grip on the cliff, as I shook in my terror. When Tex noticed I was looking down again, in a very urgent tone of voice, he commanded, "Mona, keep your eyes on me. Don't look down!"

In the meantime, Elton ran around the rim of the quarry, and then down the hillside. He had to run across the floor of the canyon, before he could start climbing the cliff to reach me.

When I felt his arms around me, relief swept over me. I no longer felt alone in my terror. Knowing my big brothers loved me, I felt it was now their responsibility to keep me safe!

Elton told me, "Put your left foot on my foot." I did. "Now put your right foot on my foot." I did.

When he said, "Take your right hand off the cliff, and put it on my wrist and hold tight," I was too afraid to turn loose of the cliff, and clung tightly with both hands.

Elton quietly told me, "Mona, I love you with all of my heart. I'll die before I let anything happen to you, but you'll have to trust me, and take hold of my wrist before I can help you--and hold tight."

It was such a hard decision to make. I was riddled with uncertainty. Tex was overhead coaxing me to take hold of Elton's wrist, Elton was pleading with me, but I was afraid if I did I would fall. Elton tried to convince me he would not let anything happen to me. Several long excruciating moments passed before I could take my right hand off the cliff, and grab his wrist, but I could not force myself to take my other hand off the cliff, and continued to grip it with all my strength. Elton and Tex took turns pleading with me to let go of the rock and grasp Elton's other wrist. It was hard for me to understand I would be safe only if I completely trusted my brother and allowed him to have the full responsibility. It took more pleading and coaxing from both Tex and Elton, before I could force myself to turn loose of the cliff. When I finally managed to overcome my paralyzing fear, and grabbed Elton's other wrist, with my feet firmly planted on his feet, we climbed up the side of the cliff. Where my arms were too short to reach the hand holds, my brother's arms made the difference.

Nearing the top of the cliff, Tex reached down, and pulled me to safety.

While I lay safely on the ground, my brothers, one on each side of me, started talking about what they should tell our parents, or how they should handle the situation. I lay there worried and wondering what my future was going to be like, when Daddy discovered I had disobeyed him, and could have fallen to my death. However, my brothers decided it would be the better part of valor to keep our mouths shut, and not let Mom or Dad know. They impressed on me, "We don't tattle on each other!" I breathed a sigh of relief, knowing my secret disobedience would not be passed on to the family, and Dad would never know I climbed the quarry.

DAUGHTER OF THE KING

Summer should have been a relaxing time, but my grandmother, a teacher in her youth, never forgot her love of teaching. In her home, the season became about education instead of playtime. We were having lunch when she once again tried to teach me a lesson.

"Mona, always hold your head high, throw back your shoulders and stand tall! You are descended from royalty."

"What do you mean, I am descended from royalty?"

"You are a daughter of a King."

This was heady stuff for a six-year-old to try to figure out. Grandpa just smiled and continued eating without saying a word. As I mulled over the thought that I was a daughter of a King, I realized if I was a daughter of a King, then Daddy couldn't be my father.

A few tears drifted down my face. Grandpa noticed and asked, "What's wrong, Honey?"

"My daddy is a mechanic."

"That's right. He is. And a good one, too."

"I want him to be my daddy."

"He is, Mona."

I grew thoughtful. Grandpa watched me with an amused twinkle in his eyes.

Grandma bustled around in the kitchen getting our dessert, so I directed my questions to Grandpa.

"Grandpa, did Grandma mean her father is a king?"

"No, honey. Grandma's father was not a king. He was a Quaker; however, he owned a whole town named after him."

This sounded impressive to me. Maybe that is why Grandma acted the way she did. She rarely smiled or laughed. Grandpa's daddy was a minister, and Grandpa laughed a lot. I thought I would like to have known Grandpa's daddy.

But confusion swamped me. If I was a daughter of a king and royalty, and Grandpa wasn't a king, and Grandma's father wasn't, then that meant my Daddy wasn't really my daddy. Tears rolled down my cheeks.

"Grandpa, I want Daddy to be my father."

Grandma walked in with apple pie for dessert in her hands, and heard me. In a demanding tone of voice, she exclaimed, "Of course Fay is your father. What kind of nonsense are you talking about now?"

Grandpa was enjoying himself. A big grin crept over his face. "I think you better explain to Mona how she is a daughter of a King."

Grandma tried. I'll give her that. "Mona, Jesus is your big brother. He is the Son of God, and God is the King of the Universe, and that means you're a daughter of a King."

I did not like the thought of Jesus being my big brother. I had enough big brothers. I wanted to look at Jesus' face and feel loved. In a sullen tone I voiced my thoughts.

"I don't want Jesus to be my big brother. I have enough brothers."

This was a big mistake!

"What do you mean you don't want Jesus for a big brother?"

Now from her tone of voice, I knew I was in deep water, and I didn't know how to swim.

"Mona, I am not understanding you. Explain yourself! Why wouldn't you want Jesus for an older brother? I never heard of such sacrilege! What have your parents been teaching you?"

Grandpa looked at me with sympathy, but didn't say anything in my defense. I was on my own.

"I have enough brothers," I muttered under my breath.

In a very deadly tone of voice, Grandma demanded, "Explain why you don't like your brothers?"

Now I was in trouble in a different way. In desperation, I cried, "I do love them. But Elton took the light bulb out of the socket, and then called me upstairs, and when I went to screw the bulb back in, and in the dark, I put my finger in the open socket, trying to turn the light on. I got a shock and it made me dance all over the floor. Elton and Henry laughed and laughed at me! And Billy called me to come and join the boys on top of the hill, and when I did, they told me to put my foot in a hole. When I did that, the hornets stung me, and I ran all the way home, with them chasing me and biting me all over my face and everywhere. Mama had to take all my clothes off to put baking soda all over the sting bites. Henry chased me one day and pushed me into the blackberry bushes, and I couldn't get out. Mama had to come and help take the thorns out of my clothes, 'cause they wouldn't let me loose, and it hurt! I have four brothers now, and I don't need any more brothers to torment me! I don't want Jesus to tease me, I just want him to love me, and so I don't want to be the daughter of a King."

"Mona, you are taking this too literally."

"What does literal mean?" I suspiciously asked.

"It means not exactly what you're talking about."

"You mean you told me a lie? I'm not really a daughter of a King?"

Before laying her head on the table in despair, Grandma groaned and looked at Grandpa for help. Grandpa's large tummy always bounced when he tried not to laugh. I watched in fascination as it now bounced up and down.

Grandpa finally took pity on both of us, and said, "Come here, honey, and I will try to explain what Grandma meant when she told you to walk tall, and keep your shoulders thrown back."

I walked around the table, and he lifted me onto his lap. After I snuggled down into his arms, Grandpa explained to me how Jesus was my big brother, and I was happy to learn I'm of royal blood.

"Now therefore fear ye not. I will nourish you, and your little ones. And He comforted them and spake kindly unto them."
Gen. 50:21

THE CHILDREN ARE HUNGRY

MY SISTER, LILLIAN, and her family moved home when her husband, Ray, lost his job. Dad decided this would be a good time for Mom to go back to San Francisco with him and have her teeth worked on. Life took a new turn for us.

When Fernne was in charge, she had a laid-back system. The work was done but she joined in our fun. She relaxed Mom's rules about eating at the table, as the front room was warmer than the dining room. Lillian went strictly by the rules. We ate breakfast at the breakfast table and dinner in the dining room. Lillian was more of a drill sergeant.

Our food supply had to stretch a little further with three extra mouths to feed. Lillian and Fernne became more inventive in what they cooked. Dad sent money on a weekly basis, but they had a hard time making the food last from one check to the next.

Since we had moved to the ranch in the fall, the only food Mom was able to can was applesauce and pears. We also had lots of firewood because when Dad came home, he spent time in the forest with the boys cutting up our winter's supply. Dad worried we might run out of fuel in the winter and freeze. In the city, we just turned on a knob to light the gas in the fireplace. Now we had trees to cut down, wood to haul, and kindling to split before we could have a warm kitchen and front room. The bedrooms were cold all winter. Mom warmed soapstone bricks, wrapped them in towels and slipped them into our beds before we went to bed.

Another major change took place when Lillian came home. She felt she should have the two-room cabin because she was married. It consisted of a bedroom and kitchen, so when her husband received a check, they ate in the cabin until they ran out of food. Then they joined us in the house. The four boys moved into the largest bedroom. This evicted Fernne out of the choice bedroom, and she had to move into my bedroom and share my twin-size bed. What an adjustment for all of us!

For some stupid reason, I felt Fernne could read my mind if she was behind me. I always insisted in either walking by her side, or behind her. Now we slept together, so I refused to go to sleep with her facing my back. This just amused her. After she went to sleep, I allowed myself to fall asleep. I soon discovered that when Fernne turned in her sleep, I had to turn also, for comfort sake. The only advantage to being so crowded in my bed was the warmth from another body.

One morning when we woke there was an eerie feeling in the air. It was as if I was deaf. No sound anywhere. It worried me.

"Fernne, wake up! Why is everything so quiet?"

She kept silent for a moment, and then said, "It must have snowed last night. Look out the window."

I jumped out of bed and ran to the window. Beautiful, white snow gleamed everywhere. The trees were covered, and the big flakes quietly covered the earth, bushes and trees. Excitement hit both of us, and we dressed in a hurry. Waking the boys, we dispensed with breakfast, and ran outside to play. After a rousing snow fight, we built a snowman. Vesta ran in the house and brought out one of Dad's old hats, and Everett found a scarf. Bill brought out one of Dad's broken pipes and put it in the mouth, and Fernne found two rocks in Mom's garden for the eyes. Henry stood and looked Mr. Snowman over and decided he needed some shoes and found two discarded ones.

After a snowman was built, we trooped into the house to warm up and to eat breakfast. While we were eating, Elton suggested he bring down the snow sleds from the barn. Elton and Henry took turns taking Everett and Vesta down the hill. When it was Bill's and my turn, Bill suggested, "Instead of going down the hill where the others have already gone, let's go down where the snow hasn't been marked."

Looking down the hill at the pristine snow, it sounded like a good idea to me. We took off and it was great, until we came to the bottom. We forgot the road carved into the side of the hill, and it was a thrill sailing out into space, but we landed about fifteen feet lower with a bang. I don't know about Bill, but it really hurt my tail bone. We lost our enthusiasm for sledding, and dragged our sleds up to join Lillian in the house.

The mail was not delivered that day, nor the next. The snow continued to fall. I knew our food supply was low because we had not been able to get to the store for groceries. I just didn't realize how low, until evening arrived, and Fernne and Lillian served us a pear cobbler for dinner. It was terrible. All they had to go with the pears was a little flour and sugar. We were hungry, so we ate it.

The next morning it wasn't so exciting seeing the snow still falling. We had our choice for breakfast, either applesauce or pears. Without flour, it was impossible to make either pancakes or bread. Looking out the front room window, we knew the mailman again would not be able to deliver the mail. The snow plow still had not plowed Newtown Road. We were snowbound without any way to buy food, even if we did receive a check from Dad. Lunchtime came and we ate applesauce and pears. Suppertime we dreaded. Again, we ate applesauce and pears.

Elton got up early each morning, took his gun, and went looking for a deer or anything he could bring home to feed his siblings. Each night he came home exhausted, cold, wet and tired. He wore a defeated look, as he explained how hard it was walking through the snow, falling into snowdrifts and getting wet, and not seeing any animals. Elton said, "The deer have more sense than I do. They probably have all drifted to a lower elevation."

My job was to iron for the ten of us, and Lillian and Fernne ran the kitchen. I was wondering if they had come up with anything else for us to eat, when I heard Lillian quietly whispering to Fernne, "Remember the Donner Party! We may all starve to death if this snow doesn't let up."

This was more than I wanted to hear, so I wandered back into the front room. My iron was cold, which surprised me. I went to the wall to turn on the lights and realized our electricity was off. When I brought the news to my sisters they looked at each other.

Fernne said, "Mona, better get the oil lamps out and trim the wicks."

"Fernne, I have never seen an oil lamp. What do they look like?"

She groaned and asked Lillian, "Doesn't Mom have any oil lamps?"

"I don't know. Remember, I've never lived here before, and Mom has always lived in the city. Let's search the house and see if we can find one."

They found one hidden in the back corner of the pantry, with just a little kerosene, and Lillian said, "Well, it looks like everyone will go to bed early. There is only enough kerosene to see everyone to bed."

I put the ironing away. Vesta complained, "The radio is off, and I can't hear the Lone Ranger."

This was her favorite program on the radio, and she had become addicted, but I preferred reading, and at least I didn't have to iron any more shirts for the boys. Now I could read until I went to bed. I didn't worry too much. Mom always managed to cook a good meal, so I trusted the girls would find something for us to eat, besides applesauce and pears.

The next day the snow continued to silently float down, and the boys had to shovel the sidewalk and make a path to the outhouse. Elton once more bravely put on his boots and heavy coat, and set out to see if he could find a deer. We were all tired of applesauce and pears, and we all took turns complaining. Lillian and Fernne wore serious looks, and I knew the situation was desperate.

Elton came in that evening, wet and miserable, but his bag contained birds he managed to kill. I looked them over, and noticed only one quail. By the Bible this was considered clean meat. I became horrified at the sight of the birds he had killed; blackbirds, sparrows, whatever he was able to find.

I told Lillian, "There is only one clean bird we can eat."

Lillian assured me, "Mona, you can have the quail. We'll eat the unclean birds."

Trusting her, I went back to the cozy fireplace to finish reading Zane Gray's book, "Nevada."

Soon the delicious aroma of food cooking wafted into the front room, and my mouth started watering. My sisters managed to make a bird pie, with the little flour, salt, and seasoning Mom kept in the pantry. Lillian called us into the dining room for dinner.

Mom always insisted the youngest be served first. When they served Vesta, she demanded, "What kind of bird am I eating?"

Quail was the only "clean" meat in the dish we could eat, I felt, by the Bible standards. Lillian told her, "You have quail, honey."

They next served Everett. Again the same question, "What kind of bird am I eating?" Fernne assured him, "You have a quail, dear."

Now I knew there was only one quail, and they had promised it to me, so I started getting a little upset and suspicious.

Billy asked, "What kind of bird do I have?"

The same story. I started smoldering inside. With just a little hesitation, Billy accepted his plate.

It was now my turn, and I decided to give them a chance. I really don't know what I expected, after the commotion I had made in the kitchen, but I asked the same question, "What kind of bird do I have?"

By this time, they must have been sick of the question. Lillian answered, "You have a quail, too, dear."

Lillian, Fernne, and Elton assured us they were going to eat the "unclean" birds.

I exploded. "You heathen! How can you sit there and tell me I have a quail, when there was only one quail in the whole bag? The rest are blackbirds and I don't know what else. You're lying! I'm not going to eat at the same table with you cannibals!"

With this parting comment, feeling very self-righteous, I went to the pantry and took a quart of applesauce. Getting up from the dining room table, Billy looked at his food longingly, but he was very loyal to me. He announced in a loud voice, "I'm going to eat with Mona. I'm not going to sit at the same table with the cannibals, either."

He took a quart of pears out of the pantry, and we dramatically stalked into the living room. We really felt sorry for ourselves. We commiserated with each other about our horrible brothers and sisters. Although we each wanted the quail for ourselves to ease our own conscience, yet it hurt knowing they were eating the birds Mom loved.

First Lillian came in and tried to reason with us. "You kids have to be reasonable. We are snowbound. There's no food, and even if Elton could someway magically walk through four or five feet of snow for five miles, we have no money to buy the food. We haven't received Dad's check, as the mail can't be delivered. You two need something else in your stomach besides applesauce and pears, and that's all you've had for three days. Please come eat a little."

She was logical and I knew she was right in trying to feed us, but we stubbornly refused to go and partake of their dinner.

I sniffed, as my tears ran down my face. I told her, "We would rather starve than eat God's birds."

Bill chimed in with, "In Sabbath School, we were told that God knows whenever a sparrow falls. I'm not going to eat a sparrow, and know God watched Elton shoot it."

Fernne came next, and she tried coaxing us. "You're going to get terribly hungry, and we don't know when anyone will get anything to eat again. You've had no food to eat, and God provided the birds. Mom would be very unhappy if she knew how long you have gone without eating."

She almost persuaded us. We could smell the bird pie and our mouths were watering.

It smelled delicious. But I could not face Mom, knowing how much she loved birds. I could see eating the quail, because God had fed quail to the Israelites to eat.

Elton looked discouraged. He was cold, exhausted and wet from hiking all day trying to find a deer. Coming home, he was thinking he had performed a miracle, to save his younger brothers and sisters from starving. He had expected a "hero's welcome," and thought we would be grateful and thankful. He looked as if he had been kicked in the stomach, when I stood and called them cannibals.

Everett and Vesta went on eating and licking their fingers. They looked so smug. They had the quail, and in their minds, their conscience was clear. We could hear them commenting on how good it tasted. When I heard Vesta ask if she could have my share, and Everett piped up and asked if he could have Bill's share, I almost caved in.

It was bad enough being hungry, and staging a "refusal to eat," but hearing them smacking their lips over OUR share of the food, and commenting on how delicious it tasted, didn't help. Henry came in once to try to talk us into eating, took one look at our stubborn faces, and left the room without saying anything. Ray and Elton left us alone in our misery.

Our older siblings really worried Bill and I might starve to death.

The snow was still coming down. Elton had a hard time finding these birds. Lillian and Fernne decided we had carried this nonsense on long enough.

Lillian announced in her drill sergeant's voice, "You two have gone as long as you're going to with just applesauce or pears. You're going to lose weight. I'm not going to have Dad tell me I allowed his two children to starve."

In a more pleading tone of voice, Fernne said, "Please come in and eat just a little of it, so you won't lose all of your strength. God has provided these birds so you won't starve."

In a very self-righteous tone, I informed them, "We are going to pray God will provide something for us to eat, and it won't be his songbirds."

Lillian came back with, "You just do that. But you will eat tomorrow, if Elton can find any more birds."

Fernne quietly commented, "Prayer always helps."

When they left the room, Bill and I knelt down in the front room and prayed God would provide food for us, as we were tired of applesauce and pears.

Around midnight, we heard a knock on the door. We all climbed out of bed and rushed to see who had made it to our house through all the snow. Ray's elderly father stood there, exhausted, and looking wet and miserable. He was so tired and cold he was shaking. Lillian and Fernne dragged him in by the stove, and Ray started building the fire. Ray fired one question after another at him, "Dad, what are you doing here in the middle of the night and during a snow storm? Where's your car? How far did you walk? Has the snow plow finally cleared the highway?"

Dad Welsh drew a deep breath, and said, "No, the roads are still closed. Highway 50 hasn't been cleared of snow. I don't know how I made it as far as I did. The snow is coming down heavy, and I couldn't see. All I knew was a voice kept telling me, "The children are hungry." I just kept driving straight ahead, until finally I was stuck and couldn't go any further. The car is about one mile below

Merrymans. I had to walk and make my own path the last two miles. Your mother and I have been worried about you, knowing this was the worst snow storm to hit in years. But it was the craziest thing. Every time I tried to go to sleep, I heard a voice say, "The children are hungry." I tried to ignore it, but the voice got louder and persistent, "The children are hungry." I finally told your Mom what I was hearing, and she was worried about me taking off in the middle of the night. It is raining heavy in Lodi, and she knew I would be facing a snow storm in the mountains, but she agreed, "It must be God talking, you'll have to go."

I went to the corner grocery store and banged on his door until I woke him up, and then when he called down from his window, "What the h— do you want?" I told him what I kept hearing, so he agreed God must be talking to me, and the grocery man got dressed, and came downstairs and helped load the car with staples. I'm too tired to walk back to the car, but you'll find it stranded on the highway below Merrymans. You won't have any trouble finding it. I don't suppose you have any coffee to drink?"

"No, Dad Welsh, but we do have some Postum left."

"I think I'd like a cup, and then could I go to bed? I'm very tired."

Henry spoke up, "Dad Welsh, you can have my bed, and I'll sleep on the couch." He turned to Elton and Ray. "Guys, let's take the sleds down to the car and bring up the food. I'm hungry, how about you?"

We all cheered in our excitement.

"Hurry up, hurry up!" Bill and I yelled. "We're starving!"

Lillian and Fernne looked at each other with relief. I think they were really afraid we were going to starve. With a nice roaring fire going, the kitchen was now warm. After Dad Welsh drank his Postum, they showed him where he could go to bed. In just a few moments, we heard poor Dad Welsh snoring.

Henry, Elton and Ray bundled up, grabbed the snow sleds and took off in the dark. About four hours later, they arrived home. They had potatoes, beans, macaroni, rice, catsup, hot sauce, coffee, eggs, bread, flour, shortening, oatmeal, pancake flour, syrup, butter, peanut butter, cheese, jam, dried cereal, a gallon of milk and even a couple bags of candy for Everett and Vesta. Lillian and Fernne immediately started peeling the potatoes to fry, and fixed a bowl of eggs to make an omelet. The aroma of fresh coffee soon filled the air. They made peanut butter and jam sandwiches for all of us, and we wolfed them down.

Bill and I were insufferable. We went around reminding then, "See, we told you God would provide food. He didn't want his birds eaten."

The rest of the family were so glad to see food again, they put up with our self-righteous and obnoxious behavior. We felt fully justified, because God did provide food for all of us, once we prayed and asked for his help.

However, it was a wonder the family spoke to us the rest of the winter.

FALLING FOR THE BUS DRIVER

IT WAS NEARLY A WEEK since my sister had absconded with my date, and I had not forgiven her betrayal. She seemed surprised we were not back on good terms, as if in her mind, nothing serious had happened.

This had created a very strained atmosphere in our family. My brothers showed their support by joining me as we all gave Fernne the silent treatment. We would get up and walk out of the room if she entered it. It made for some very tense family meals.

Mom asked me to go in the bedroom, as she wanted to have a little chat with me.

"Your sister is sorry for her actions and for hurting you. She wants you to forgive her."

I remained silent.

"Your brothers won't until you do. They are completely loyal to you."

Good!

"What Fernne did was reprehensible, but I hope she has learned a lesson."

"I doubt it."

"Can't you forgive her?"

"She hasn't asked me to forgive her, Mom, in case you haven't noticed."

Mom was silent. I don't think she knew how to respond. Finally she said, "Jesus told us in the Lord's Prayer, we must forgive others the way we want God to forgive us. I know this is a hard thing to do when she hurt you so deeply."

"I don't even know what to say to her. I feel sick when I look at her."

"Mona, I can't have a house divided. You can't go on treating Fernne like she doesn't exist. Remember, she was kidnapped when she was two years old. I believe this affected her more than we realized."

After a few seconds passed, Mom continued, "One way to prevent this in the future would be for you to always suggest your dates bring a friend along to keep your sister's attention occupied."

I wasn't too keen about forgiving Fernne, but I was getting tired of looking through her, and keeping up the battle lines. It was exhausting to stay so angry. I told Mom, "I'll speak to her at breakfast tomorrow morning. Let her stew one more day."

Mom sighed. She was hoping for immediate peace in her family, but at least she had a partial victory. She got up from my bed where she had been sitting, and leaning over, kissed me on the forehead. "Thank you, Honey. You know I love you with all my heart."

The next morning, when I reached the breakfast table, Fernne looked at me with a wistful smile. I said, "Good morning, Fernne," and waited to see what her reaction would be.

She looked up at me with almost pathetic gratitude. "Good morning, sweetie."

I could feel the tension leave the breakfast table. The boys were soon themselves, bickering and teasing. I wasn't very talkative as it was still hard for me to even be in the same room with her, but things did get better among all of us.

Summer was over and we prepared ourselves for school. I dreaded this. School was going to be so completely different. I had attended a large school, and El Dorado High School was small in comparison. Bill, Everett and Vesta were going to be attending a two-room schoolhouse at Smith Flat. I couldn't even imagine what life was going to be like for them. I was appalled when I found out they had four grades in one room. How backwards could this school district be? I asked Dad, "How are we going to get to school each day? There are no streetcars here."

Dad smiled at my ignorance and patiently told me, "You will be riding school buses."

"What is that like?"

He smiled and tried to find a parallel I would understand.

"They are like the Greyhound bus."

This didn't tell me anything, as I had never ridden on a Greyhound bus. I loved riding streetcars, and even hanging onto the straps with my body swaying as the streetcar sped along. The unknown was something I dreaded.

Climbing on the school bus Monday morning, I was nervous until Edna called out, "Mona, I've saved a seat for you."

I joined Edna in the seat she saved and thanked her.

"Are you speaking to Fernne yet?"

"I had to. My mother had a big talk with me about forgiving her."

Edna looked at me and shook her head. "I'm still not speaking to Clint after what they pulled."

Somehow this made me feel better.

I decided to run Mom's idea by her. "My mother suggested whenever I have a date, to always see if my boy friend could bring along one of his friends to distract Fernne."

She grew thoughtful, and then said, "I think I'll ask George to drive me to your house after this instead of Clint."

This sounded like an excellent idea. Her brother George was our school bus driver. In his twenties, this tall, dark and handsome Texan was closer to Fernne's twenty-two years than his brother Clint. He didn't smile a lot, but when he did, it was loaded with warmth. He had an air of quiet strength about him and always made me feel safe in his company.

When George came to visit us in the evenings, he was our friend and we called him by his first name. On the bus he was Mr. Gardner, and we respected him. He only had to tell the troublemakers they would have to walk to school if they didn't behave, and they straightened right up. There was only once he ever made a boy get off and walk. Roy liked to use bad language and George, true to his word, kicked him off the bus. After two weeks I think Roy grew tired of trudging to high school and seeing all of us in the bus pass him by. Roy never swore on the bus again.

Elton was out of high school, and Dad could not afford to send him to college. Elton did not have a job, so he had a tendency to be a gypsy and roam. He was always taking off to visit our grandparents in Lodi, and his girlfriend Betty in Stockton. With Dad in San Francisco during the week, Henry felt the full responsibility of keeping the ranch running. He also milked the cow and strained the milk before going to school. Billy kept Mom's wood box full, and our little brother Everett helped out by gathering the eggs.

My job was making lunches for my four siblings and myself. Five lunches, with four sandwiches for Henry's alone, were a lot to make out of homemade bread. Sometimes in cutting the bread, I made the slices too thick. Henry and Bill would complain that I made the sandwiches so thick it was like trying to put a half a loaf of bread in their mouth.

My sister, Vesta, was our little 'gofer'. I would yell, "Vet, I can't find my algebra book, will you get it?"

Bill would sing out, "Vet, bring me my baseball," or Henry would call, "Vet, I can't find my boots."

She was the pet of all of us, and she was eager to please. We adored her, and let her tag along, but we also took complete advantage of her desire and willingness to be with us.

When Edna and her brothers, John and Richard, came to visit, we would go in the front room and play games. Several months passed before Clint ever came to the ranch to visit again. He acted his usual charming self, and appeared not to understand why he could not talk me into going out with him.

George would come up two to three times a week to visit with Fernne. He would smile that slow sexy smile of his and drawl, "Fernne, I could smell your homemade bread down the road as I was driving the bus, and it drew me up here like a bee to honey."

They enjoyed sitting in the kitchen with their feet propped up into the oven-door and just visiting. It seemed as if they could talk for hours. I think because of the Clint fiasco, George made it clear he just wanted to be her friend. I often thought it was a shame she had made a play for Clint first, as George and she were so compatible.

Meanwhile, poor Henry had little time for visiting. One of the most time consuming aspects of running the ranch for him was rounding up the cow to milk her. This always added a little excitement, especially in the morning, as we would wait to see him come running down from the barn, covered with leaves and debris from having to go into the orchard to bring Bossy home. Our fences were weak from years of neglect, and all Bossy had to do to escape would be to wrap her head around one wire and jerk to loosen the fence enough to get through.

After he was through milking the cow, he would dash down the hill to change his clothes, yelling, "Mom, you'll have to strain the milk. Vet, get my books. Mona, bring my lunch, Eb, have my boots handy."

We all ran to do our assigned chores, knowing he would never make the bus without our help. It never entered any of our minds that Henry should get up earlier than we did, to go look for the cow.

George had made the mistake one day of telling us, "As long as I can see someone coming, I can keep the bus waiting for you."

Of course, this meant a few times everyone on the bus was late for school.

Our ranch was known as Poplar Knoll Ranch from all the poplar trees growing around the rim. One aspect of living at the top of the mountain was sound traveled up to where we lived. We could hear the bus coming one-half mile away, so when Mom could hear the bus coming around the curve approaching our ranch, she would send Vesta down the hill first. George would be able to see her at the bus stop, so he would slow the bus, to pick her up.

Everett, waiting on top for the bus to stop for Vesta, would start down the steps as she got on the bus. After he got to the bottom, it would be my brother Bill's turn to start running. I would be standing on the top of our little bridge spanning the creek, and when I saw him enter the door of the bus, it would be my turn. This always gave Henry time to change his clothes and run out of the door. George never left without all of the West children, unless we told him one of us was sick.

Whoever cleared the mountain for a ranch, before we moved there, had cut approximately seventy-five steps in the side of the steep hill. These steps were terraced, some had three steps in between each terrace, some had five steps and a few had two or four. This meant you had to watch your feet coming down. The top to the bottom of the mountain was over one hundred fifty feet.

One day as I ran down the steps, I made the mistake of looking at the bus instead of watching my feet. Suddenly, with no warning, I lost my balance and the whole world turned upside down. The next instant I flew through the air. Somehow, the exhilaration of soaring down the mountain overrode the panic I should have felt at what was sure to be my imminent demise.

When my flight ended with a crash behind a manzanita bush at the bottom, I did not have a single bruise or hurt any place on my body. I should have been dead, or at the very least had massive injuries. The wind wasn't knocked out of me. Moving each arm and each leg, they proved to be in fine shape. I felt like God had gently laid me down. Later, my Dad told me from where I had nosedived off, I fell the equivalent of seven floors.

Meanwhile, Henry, being the last one to the bus as usual, missed the entire thing. He ran down the side, watching the steps with care as he always did. When he climbed on the school bus, I heard George start yelling at him.

"Henry, Mona just fell all the way down from the top of the steps. I can't believe you didn't stop to check on her. I saw the whole thing. I'm afraid she might be dead."

Some of the children were crying, and others were praying out loud. Henry backed out of the bus, and ran frantically to the spot George pointed out to him where I would be. When he got to the bushes, expecting to see me dead or unconscious, he couldn't believe his eyes. He found me looking up at the heavens, with a big smile on my face. Henry went from terrified to enraged in a matter of seconds.

"What do you think you are doing?" he roared.

"I'm looking up at the clouds," I replied, stating the obvious.

His panic for my safety turned into misplaced anger, and grabbing me by my arm he pulled me up.

"Do you realize not only George, but all the kids on the bus think you're dead?"

My peaceful moment over, he marched me to George where I had to apologize for scaring him.

George asked me with concern, "Are you sure your back doesn't hurt? What about your head? Mona, you don't have to go to school today if you hurt anywhere." He kept staring at me like he couldn't believe his eyes.

When I went to my seat, I sat by Vesta. She looked at me with the admiring eyes of a little sister. "Mona, did you know you did a complete somersault in the air? How did you do it? Can you do it again? Can I try it tomorrow?"

I switched into big sister mode and told her, "Are you crazy? NO!"

Vesta crossed her arms and pouted. "You get to have all the fun."

***

56

I sent this chapter to George for verification, and he told me this was just the way he remembered it. He had told this amazing story to his grandchildren many times, and some of them didn't believe it, so he was happy to get my written story of the event, to justify him in his grandchildren's eyes.

I found it interesting when I asked my sons, brothers, and various in-laws how far it was up the hill, they told me from 100 feet to 250 feet. When I asked how many stairs there were, they told me from 50 to well over 100 steep stairs. Each one had a different number. Only my son Larry and I agreed it was 98 steps.

WORSHIP AT THE RANCH

MY SISTER, FERNNE, had been kidnapped by her father and aunt when she was two. She was told so many lies by her aunt; she had no desire to ever see her mother again. Years later, when Fernne's father started coming back to see his son, Elton, and his daughter, Lillian, she refused to come with him (or so he said).

Poor Mom. She longed for her baby so much. She had a small photo of Fernne, so one day, after she married my Dad, he took the photo of Lillian and Fernne to an artist, and he painted a large picture of them for mom as a surprise. Mom prayed for all of us, but I noticed when she prayed for Fernne, her voice would sound as if it were full of tears.

One day, when I came home from high school, as I walked into the front room, I noticed a young lady in a deep conversation with my mom. They both looked at me, and I knew Mom wanted me to be quiet and go into the kitchen. After the young lady left, my mother came out and told me with a serious look, "That was your sister, Fernne. She had a lot of questions she wanted answers to." Now I knew what my sister, Fernne, looked like, as an adult.

Fernne wrote to my oldest sister, Lillian, and then started writing to Mom. About a year later, when we moved to the ranch, Fernne drove up, and moved home. I wasn't sure at first whether I liked having an older sister at home to tell me what to do. I was very happy having two older brothers and two younger brothers and a baby sister. I could convince Vesta there was a boogie man in the closet or under the bed, and she better be quiet, and not tattle to Daddy or Momma that I was reading a book after the lights were suppose to be off or the boogie man might get her.

Poor Vesta. She told me on her honeymoon, she looked under her bed from force of habit. Her husband, Elder Don Mansell, asked her, "Vesta, why are you looking under the bed?" She arose with a red face. He grinned and told her, "Honey, from now on. I'll protect you. You don't have to look under the bed for a boogie man." I felt so ashamed of myself. I had no idea she believed me that much, while growing up.

Now I had an older sister who I thought could read my mind and tell me what to do, if she could see the back of my head. For example, she would ask me what I was going to do about my boyfriend situations, just as I was trying to figure out what to do about Tommy. It was a weird feeling and I was not happy about her knowing what I was thinking. She laughed at me when I made sure I faced her, or was walking along the side of her. I refused to walk in front of her, which amused her to no end.

For one thing, I spent a good portion of my time always trying to be in front facing her. I thought I could keep her from reading my mind if I faced her. I know the family thought I was going through an awkward stage. I was forever tripping, trying to get in front of her instead of letting her stand behind me. Try sometime; see what happens when you never let one particular person in the family walk behind you. They are always saying "You go first, Mona." I didn't want to go first. I wanted to be last.

To make matters worse, my sister Lillian moved home with her husband and baby son, so Fernne had to give up living in the cabin, and let Lillian and her husband move into the cabin, which meant Fernne had no place to sleep except with me. I insisted on sleeping behind her so she could not read my mind!

Life was full of fun and lots of laughter at our ranch, with eight children. The other two ranches had nine and ten children respectively, and it seemed as if we had a party every Saturday night between us.

I don't want to give the impression Fernne was a drill sergeant. If we came up with a wild idea, Fernne generally joined in.

Winters were cold in Placerville, and we had never experienced living in a snow country before. So with the only heat in the house a wood stove that barely heated the kitchen and a fireplace that only heated one-half the front room, we became innovative. I am not sure if it was Henry's idea or Billy's, but when we came home from school, Fernne was sitting in by the front room fire trying to keep warm, and she had an iron pot hanging by a hook suspended over the fire, with beans simmering. They weren't done. We were hungry. So Henry went in the cold kitchen and got some canned pork and beans and put them in the hot coals.

In about fifteen minutes they were beginning to bulge, and he raked them out, and we ate a hot dinner. We figured we could eat Fernne's dinner later. That became a simple way of eating from then on. We would figure out how many cans we needed, roll them in the fireplace, and then eat out of the can. This also saved washing dishes.

I should explain about the pork and beans. True, pigs are unclean animals, but for some reason, we felt if we took out the pork and didn't eat it, we could eat the beans. We never thought about the pork fat that leached into the beans while they were cooked. With that mindset, we were able to eat them with a clear conscience.

One night, while waiting for them to get warm, we got to playing Rook. In the excitement of the game, we forgot to fish our cans of pork and beans out, and they exploded all over the front room. What a mess. We were ducking not only the hot metal, but the beans as they shot out of the can. This didn't deter us any from our practice.

Once, we had hot soup explode all over the front room. Fernne laughed as much as we did, and we all pitched in cleaning up the ceiling, walls, floors, and put six more cans in for dinner. This time we watched them closer. It was Vesta's and Everett's job to let us know if they started to expand.

Fernne baked homemade bread about every other day, and on those days we had a nice hot kitchen to come home to.

Our high school bus driver, George Gardner, was also my best friend, Edna's, brother. He maintained he could smell Fernne's bread baking as he would drive by. He always seemed to be there as she took the bread out of the oven. She would serve him cold milk and hot homemade bread. They sat around the wood stove in the kitchen, with the oven door open, kitchen lights out, and quietly talk. The kitchen door was always open, so we could come and go as we pleased.

George was a friendly, handsome young man about twenty-five to thirty years old. He must have stood over six feet tall. He had dancing blue eyes that crinkled at the corners. His father owned the ranch about one mile east of us. They were from Texas and they all talked with a soft Texas drawl. George teased and joked with us. The next morning, when we got on the bus, we went back to being very "respectful" to "Mr. Gardner".

George and Fernne had a warm, close friendship—Nothing like a boyfriend-girlfriend—just a nice, wholesome friendship. On rainy nights, it was very comforting knowing there was a man in the house, even if he would be going home around midnight. Elton wasn't home evenings very often, and Henry was only sixteen, so I looked forward to George's visits.

On Sabbath morning, Fernne went to each bedroom, and insisted we get up and dress for church. With no transportation, this meant walking five miles over curving mountain roads. I informed Fernne, "Now that I am fourteen, I have decided I don't have to walk to church any more. I have decided to sleep in."

I am not sure how Fernne managed it. I must have dosed back off to sleep, because I woke up on the floor with half the bedding with me. We slept in a twin bed. Someway she managed to get behind me and leaning her back to the wall, she managed to kick me out and on to the floor. I know I had a shocked look on my face. Fernne told me, "Mona, you are not going to grow up be a heathen! Get up off the floor and get ready for church." Then she softened the blow with, "I have noticed your Sabbath dress is old, and my clothes are all new. Go to my closet, and pick out any dress you want, and you may wear it to church. From now on, my closet is your closet on Sabbath."

"Wow!" I was up off the floor in a flash! I knew what dress I wanted to wear, and she smiled as I put it on. After that, each Sabbath she enticed me with, "What dress are you going to wear to church today?" She actually seemed happy seeing me in her dresses. What a wonderful sister she turned out to be!

Walking up and down hills, we soon developed muscles' in our legs, as we all got ready for church. Getting us ready for church was one thing; keeping us clean was another. We gave Fernne a bad time going to church. First Everett would wander off, throwing rocks down the hill. Next Billy declared a sit-down strike. He sat down on a rock, and said, "I am tired and I am not walking another step."

I am not sure how she managed to get Billy up and walking again. I know I was glad of the rest of hiking up that mountain, but soon she had Billy back on the road. Then she noticed only Billy, Everett, Vesta, and myself were with her. Henry kept walking. He was almost out of sight around a curve, when Fernne started yelling for him to wait for us. He stopped, but I knew my brother well enough to know he was sizzling inside and wishing he wasn't one of us.

After I noticed Billy and Everett were having a lot of fun, I joined in. I started throwing rocks also. This brought the wrath of Fernne down on my head.

"Mona, what do you think you're doing?"

I tried to play innocent. Grinning, I turned around and told her, "Just throwing rocks with the boys. You ought to try it, Fernne; did you know I can throw a rock as far as Billy?"

She was not amused. "Mona, you are supposed to set an example for Vesta! How is she going to know how to behave like a lady? Look at her! She is getting dirty!"

Then a screech came out of Fernne. "Henry, get Everett! He is getting dirty sitting in the dirt!"

Back to the road I went, holding Vesta's hand as long as she allowed me to. Vesta's inclination was, "If Everett can do it, I can." However, she minded better than either me or the boys. We were always late for Sabbath School, but Fernne usually got us there maybe only ten minutes late.

The Adventist families who passed us in cars with room to spare never stopped and offered rides to any of us. Fernne finally had words with one of the elders who passed us with room for three or four of us. She told him the least he could do was give Everett, Vesta and Billy a ride. He did one day, then started leaving for church earlier, before we walked passed his house, so he could claim he didn't see us.

Fernne became indignant about it, but reconciled he was not willing to share his car with children.

Mom was sick and in San Francisco for around a year, and considering the fact that Fernne had never seen any of us, except that one glimpse of me, I think she did a pretty good job raising us.

There was another way Fernne changed things. When Mom was home, she was so busy with all of us children there was rarely time for worship. Worship at Grandpa Sander's house was a warm experience. When he read the "begets," it was music in my ears, and when he read from the book of Psalms, it gave me a love for the book of Psalms I have today. His voice was melodious. He read one chapter and then prayed. It was a pleasure to hear him pray.

Worship at Aunt Beulah's was an ordeal. She read long chapters out of the book, *Great Controversy*. When we knelt to pray she prayed for everyone in the family. Every relative! It was nice that she prayed for my seven brothers and sisters, and her own three children, but then she continued praying for her brothers and their wives and their children.

When she prayed for my great-aunts and great-uncles, and even for people I didn't know, I squirmed. My knees ached. My back hurt. I hated it. I did my level best never to be at Aunt Beulah's house near worship time, but she seemed to have it at a different time each day, and I was always getting there in time for it. What was worse, they always had everyone present say a prayer, and I dreaded it when she or Uncle Amos said, "Mona, it's your turn."

All I ever learned to say was Now I Lay Me Down To Sleep or The Lord's Prayer. How was I going to say that in front of all of her family? They all seemed to pray different. I hated it. It was embarrassing and made me cringe inside. When she told me it was my turn, I stumbled around trying to pray like Grandpa did, and doing it so low no one could hear me, knowing I was making a mess of it, and then loudly saying "Amen".

Uncle Amos complained that he could never hear what I was saying when I prayed. I certainly didn't want anyone to hear me! Sometimes I said the Lord's Prayer, and then they all had to join in. I also was afraid I would forget the words to the Lord's Prayer before the others joined in and wouldn't that be humiliating!

I didn't' want to pray out loud and have them make fun of me later like we did Vesta. When it was her turn, she said, "God bless all the missionaries in the cornfield." She thought this was what people were praying when Aunt Beulah or Uncle Amos prayed for "the missionaries in the foreign field." She was only five and really smart for her age, but I sure didn't want them teasing me about my "Now I lay me," so I purposely mumbled.

When Fernne announced, "We are going to start having Sundown Worship," I groaned. I complained. Fernne said, "Mona, you're a heathen, and it is time you participated in worship".

Ever since Fernne kicked me out of bed when I announced, "I'm sleeping in, because after all I'm fourteen now, and I don't have to go to church anymore," I knew better then to argue with her. She'd just find a way to make me do it! I seethed inside over worship; reasoning with her was not successful. "Fernne, I'm not a heathen! Mom didn't' always have worship, and if Mom didn't have it, I don't see why we should have it."

Fernne stood and flashed her big brown eyes at me. "I am not criticizing Mom. She's been too busy to have it and she's been sick. I'm not sick, and if you kids did your share of work, there would be plenty of time for worship."

When night time came, Fernne hit us with, "It's time for worship." I was right in the middle of a good novel, a *Zane Grey,* and she expected me to put it down and listen to her read something religious! I sure didn't see why Mom had to stay away so long. She always allowed me to finish the chapter I was reading before I had to do whatever she wanted. Not Fernne. When she said, "It's time," we had to stop what we were doing.

Whenever a letter arrived from Mom or Dad, Fernne gathered us around her when we got home from school, and would read it to us. Then she would insist we all write a letter to them. This helped us so we were able to handle our homesickness for them.

Fernne also surprised me when she said, "Okay, let's gather around the piano." I was wondering, *How do we gather around the piano?* It stood with the back to the wall. She started playing hymns and we sang. We all loved singing hymns and a thought crossed my mind, "Hey—this is great. She has forgotten to have worship! If we sing long enough, maybe she will forget to read a whole chapter out of *The Great Controversy.* Fernne had a beautiful contralto voice, Elton sang baritone, Henry sang tenor, and Bill, Everett, Vesta and I carried the melody. (Elton later sang in operas). The others must have had the same idea, because they each picked out their favorite songs to sing, and we sang until we were all tired and happy.

When we stopped singing, she said, "Let's kneel down and thank God that Mom is alive and getting well." This sounded pretty good. We all knelt down and we each said a small prayer thanking God, and then we got up. I kept waiting for the clincher of seeing her pull out

The Great Controversy. Vesta asked, "Fernne, when are we going to have Sundown Worship? I'm tired and I want to go to bed."

"Why, Honey child, you've just had it. Good night."

Vesta was as amazed as I was. She asked me while getting ready for bed, "I thought you were supposed to pray and pray and pray when you have worship?"

I told her, "We always did at Aunt Beulah' but Fernne seems to do things different, and I like her way of worship."

Fernne seemed to find other ways for Sundown Worship. One night we played guessing games; "Who knows the name of Jacob's wife?" "Who was the man who betrayed Jesus?" She seemed to know what questions to ask so Vesta and Everett knew the answers when it was their turn and she asked harder questions when it was Henry, Bill or my turn, "What are the names of Jesus' brothers? And who has gone to heaven without seeing death?"

We never dreaded worship again. I looked forward to the evenings when we "gathered around" the piano and sang hymns. I enjoyed the nights we played the Bible games, and I found I actually listened to the words as she read out of *The Great Controversy,* as she sometimes just read half the chapter. I never dreaded Worship again, and I have always been thankful to my sister, Fernne, for teaching me how to pray to Jesus.

"Call unto me and I will deliver thee."
Jeremiah 33:3

ONE INCH FROM ETERNITY

DURING WORLD WAR II, because of gas rationing, the government had a slogan: "Is This Trip Really Necessary?" Gasoline was scarce, so when we went to town, the government told us to pick up our neighbors. Tires were also rationed, and we were only allowed retreads. Soon, many tires had retreads on top of retreads.

We lived on an isolated ranch five miles from Placerville, California, served by a narrow, twisty, mountain road. Most of the men in the community were serving in the military on active duty. The few men not on active duty were frozen to jobs necessary for the war effort.

My husband served on a destroyer tender in the South Pacific. My father worked in San Francisco repairing the oil burners for our destroyers and battleships. One day, he was thrilled to find the oil burner he was working on was designated for the destroyer my brother Bill was on, the *U.S.S. Robinson*.

This destroyer was in every major battle in the Pacific Ocean. My brother wrote home regularly to us, assuring us he was safe, and not to worry about him, as he never saw any action. We realized he was saying this to reassure Mom when we saw a newsreel with his ship's guns blazing away. The newscaster stated, "This destroyer is called the 'Lucky Robinson' because it has been in every major battle since Sipan without sustaining any serious damage." My brother Elton served under General Rose in the tank corps in Germany, and my brother Henry landed on D-Day in France. He was a medic in the 16th Infantry, 1st Division.

Henry bought a Model A Ford coupe before he entered the army. With all the men gone, I became the designated driver for four families, as the other women could not drive. The rationing board gave me gas coupons so I would be able to drive each woman to town for groceries or to their doctor. Some days, I found myself making two trips.

One day, it was necessary to drive to town for groceries, and I crowded in my twelve-year-old sister, Vesta. She held my three-year-old son Harold on her lap, and my infant son, Larry, in her arms. I picked up my neighbor, Dora Ebbert, who also held her infant son Donald in her arms, and her toddler son, Henry, also three, on her lap. It was a good thing we all were thin.

My girlfriend Dora enjoyed teasing me by saying she wasn't sure there was a God. She said, "I guess I'm an agnostic. I don't know what to believe." I tried to convince her there was a God who loved and protected us, but she just grinned and said, "You'll have to prove it to me."

That day, while driving to Placerville for our weekly groceries, the right front tire blew out as we were going around a curve. We were heading for the cliff, and I knew if we went over, we would all be killed. This was before power steering. I tried with all my strength to turn the steering wheel, but with the flat tire, I wasn't strong enough. In my terror I called out, "Oh, God, help me!"

Instantly, I felt a pair of strong hands on my wrists that helped me turn the wheel. When I got the car stopped, I leaned my head on the steering wheel, and thanked God. My whole body was shaking like a leaf.

Vesta asked, "What happened, Mona?"

I held up my wrists and exclaimed, "Vesta, look! Look!"

We could see the finger imprints on my wrists.

We got out of the car and looked at how close we came to the precipice. The tire marks in the dirt showed we drove on the very edge of the cliff, just one inch from eternity. Kneeling down in the dirt, each of us thanked God for delivering us from death. Vesta and Dora were especially impressed with the fingerprints on my wrists.

After changing the tire, a task at which I had become very proficient, we climbed back into the car and drove to Placerville without further incident.

When we arrived in Placerville, the fingerprints were still on my wrists. We parked in the Purity parking lot and walked into the store. Dora called out, "Everyone, come look at Mona's wrists! Let me tell you what happened."

As the customers crowded around, Dora told them how close we came to dying, and how she heard me call out, "Oh, God, help me!" And God did!

The customers looked at my wrists, and some of them wanted to touch the prints.

Dora dragged us down Main Street into each store. She was so overjoyed at being alive, and knowing there was a God, she wanted to tell everyone in town. Sometimes she allowed Vesta to tell the story and how she felt about it. We covered the whole town, and the marks stayed firmly imbedded as a witness to our miracle. The imprints faded after we had covered the town testifying to what God had done for us. That night, I lay in bed and looked at my now smooth wrists, marveling how God loved us enough to perform miracles like he did in Biblical days.

Many times, I wondered why our lives were spared so dramatically, until Vesta grew up and married a young minister. They served as missionaries in Brazil and Thailand. Don and Vesta now write devotional and inspirational books. I felt this was the reason God spared our lives.

My son Larry, who was a baby in Vesta's arms, became a minister. He joined the army as a chaplain, jumped with the paratroopers into Panama during our invasion, and won medals for saving lives. I felt this was another reason our lives were spared.

Dora accepted Jesus as her Savior and attended church regularly, raising her children in her faith. She is no longer an agnostic. Now she knows there is a God.

I know God loves me, too. My guardian angel and I have been involved in many miraculous events. My experiences have confirmed my belief that God wants me to tell others to encourage them, so they may get to know and love Him, as I do.

One of my favorite verses in the Bible is Jeremiah 33:3: "Call on Me and I will answer."

***

This happened in 1943, and I will never forget it. Vesta has told this story many times in church. Dora told me she will never forget the horror of thinking she was going to die, and when she saw the handprints on my wrists, all doubts were gone, and she knew there was a God.

My brothers were Elton Adams—who was a Sergeant under General Rose, and drove tanks, Henry West— who was a PFC medic who landed on D-Day (1st Co, 16 Inft, 1st Div) and was killed by our own airplanes who dropped bombs on our troops on August 1, 1944. My brother Norman "Bill" West was a Fire Control Petty Officer 2nd Class. He operated the computer that controlled and aimed the firing of the large guns.

My husband was Harold Smedley, who was First Class Seaman in the Navy.

My father was Fay West, who built oil burners for destroyers, at Ray Oil Burner co.

ROLLING STOP

DICK MIARS WAS TWELVE when his family moved to the bottom of the hill where we lived in a remote area. After his mother obtained work in Washington, D.C., as a single parent, she was forced to leave her children at home alone. Isabelle, aged sixteen; Charley—known as Dude—was fifteen; Jim, fourteen; Dick, twelve; Dan, ten; and Johnny, eight, were all left with no supervision, except for my mother. Dick and my brother, Bill, thirteen years old, became inseparable and were always into mischief. Soon all of them were eating at our home, and we grew up as brothers and sisters.

After World War Two broke out, Mrs. Miars returned to California to work for McClellan Air Force Base, and bought a home in Sacramento. Isabelle (Izzy) joined the WAC. Dude joined the Army, Jim and Dick joined the Marines, and Dan joined the Air Force.

Before the war, ladies seldom learned to drive. When the government froze my father to his job and my brothers were either drafted or joined the service, it was imperative I learn to drive a car.

Lonely with all of her children in the service except for Johnny, Mrs. Miars asked me to move to Sacramento. Married children lived with their parents, and garages were turned into homes. Houses for rent were next to impossible to find, but Mrs. Miars managed to locate a house for me one block from where she lived. When Dick received a medical discharge from the Marines, he moved home. My husband received his medical discharge from the Navy around the same time. They both found work driving cement trucks, but on different shifts.

With gasoline rationed, Mrs. Miars insisted Dick pick me up to go grocery shopping each time he'd shop for her. This helped me immensely. However, I noticed Dick glanced to his right and pulled out onto the highway without slowing down. I protested, "Dick, you didn't stop at the stop sign. That's against the law!"

Laughing, he replied, "That's called a California Rolling Stop."

"But Dick, that's against the law!"

"No cop is going to give you a ticket for that."

I mulled over what he said. It didn't sound safe to me, but each day this was the way he drove me to the store.

While Dick was at work one day, I decided to drive to the store to buy some ingredients for the meal I was preparing. My sons, Harold and Larry, were toddlers, and I was pregnant with my daughter, Gloria Jean. I piled my sons in the back seat of my car and started for the store. When I came to the stop sign, my conscience bothered me but I decided this one time, to follow Dick's example.

After I reached the end of the street, I shifted into second, looked to the right, and not seeing any cars, drove onto the highway. There was a curve I could not see around, and I was driving too slowly to enter the highway. I glanced into my rear-view mirror and became terrified. A large cement truck with a full load in the rolling drum was almost on top of me. This was prior to seat belts; my boys were standing up and shouting "Uncle Dick! Uncle Dick!"

Just before he rolled over us, he yanked the wheel to the right, jackknifing the truck. It tipped on its side. I quickly parked and ordered my sons to stay put, and then ran back to see if Dick was still alive.

When I arrived at the scene of the accident, I heard Dick calling me, "Mona, help me out of this thing. I can't seem to climb out with my head where my feet belong."

After clambering up the side of the truck, I lay on my cumbersome belly, and reached down into the truck to try to reach Dick's hands, and help him to curl around to an upright position.

We stood in shock, and looked at the wreck. Dick seemed to have a bewildered air about him. Looking down at the truck, and then glancing at me, he asked, "Why in the world did you pull in front of me? I had no choice. Either run over you and the boys or wreck the truck."

While we were standing on the side of the highway looking down the embankment on the wrecked truck, my body started shaking, but I still protested, "Dick, you told me you could just do a California Rolling Stop there."

A confused look passed over his face. Sighing, he said, "Guess I need to give you some more driving lessons. Well, we better go to the store, and let me phone my boss and tell him what happened."

Dick climbed into my car and I drove on to the store. I listened as he made the telephone call. After he explained what happened, Dick became silent. I knew his job was in jeopardy and I felt sick to my stomach. When he hung up, he turned to me with a charming smile and said, "I never did like that job anyway. Let's go home, Mona."

THE MYSTERIOUS STRANGER

WHEN WORLD WAR II BROKE OUT, it created many problems for me as my husband was drafted into the Navy. Not only food, gasoline, tires, and shoes were rationed, but also affordable living quarters were difficult to find. I could not afford to live in our home without his salary. My government allotment covered the rent and utilities, but did not cover food and clothing for our two little boys. This made it necessary for me to move home to my parents' ranch.

My two sons, four-year-old Harold Jr., also known as Tootie, and my Larry, aged two, loved living with their grandparents. However, this made for a crowded household. My brother, Everett, gave me his large bedroom, so my sons and I moved into it; he slept on the couch in the front room. With both my mother and my twelve-year-old sister, Vesta, helping me to raise my toddlers, my life became easier.

When my husband received his discharge from the Navy, housing was still impossible to find, because no new houses were built during the war. We continued to live with my parents. Soon, I was expecting another little one.

The doctor agreed with my choice to deliver the baby at the ranch.

Dr. Jean Babcock had delivered my son, Larry, at the ranch also, and she was one of the few remaining doctors not in the military.

When I felt the first twinges of my baby's coming, Mom and I drove to town to see my doctor. She confirmed the baby would be born that day. I seemed to have an unlimited amount of energy, so we did some shopping, paid the bills in town, and headed home to prepare for the big event.

I moved my two little boys into my mother's bedroom, so they would not be with me during the birth of my baby. A storm was approaching, so we built a warm fire in the wood stove, and started dinner. The pains came closer together, and Mom felt we should notify the doctor.

The rain began to fall gently as my mother walked the two miles to use the telephone to call her. I wondered when Dr. Jean would arrive, and when after an hour she still had not come, Mom made another trip to the telephone. Each time Mom telephoned, the nurse assured her that Dr. Jean would be on the way. When my husband and my father came home from work, they found me pacing the floor.

Grinning, my Dad asked, "What, no baby yet?"

"Not yet, Dad—you know your grandkids have a mind of their own. They come when they're ready."

My husband, Harold, asked, "Am I going to be fed before the big event?"

I told him, "Go eat dinner. Mom has cooked it, and it's ready to put on the table. I'm afraid it's going to be a long night."

Hours later, when Dr. Jean still had not arrived, my husband and my brother decided to go search for the missing doctor. The weather by now had all the appearances of a real winter storm, and the rain was lashing against the windowpanes. I didn't envy their trip, but I was becoming worried about Dr. Jean not showing up in time to deliver my baby.

The rolling thunder and lightning flashes woke my little sons and they were terrified. They found themselves in a strange, dark bedroom. They started calling, "Mommie, Mommie."

They expected me to come to them and tell them it was all right. Normally, I sang a lullaby to them, and they drifted back to sleep, relaxed and comforted. This time, I couldn't. I found myself in hard labor. I heard them fretting, fussing, and then whimpering, and finally sobbing, "Mommie, I want a drink of water."

"Mommie can't come right now," I called to them. "Please go back to sleep."

"Mommie, please, I want a drink of water."

They continued to cry, and this upset me.

The pounding rain caused the electricity to go out. My father started lighting the candles and the kerosene lamp, and then built a warm fire in the fireplace. My mother arranged everything the doctor needed.

My mother sent Vesta from one job to another, but when she finally wandered into my bedroom, I asked her, "Vesta, please go and take the boys a glass of water."

She was happy to be able to do it, but just then Mom called and said, "Vesta, I need your help."

Vesta had become everyone's "go for." When Vesta later came into my bedroom, I asked her, "Did you take them a glass of water? I noticed they've quit crying."

Her face seemed to have a glow; however, she wore a bewildered expression. "They have a glass of water."

"Who gave it to them?"

"They said the man in white."

I replied, "Vesta, no cars have driven up the hill- we'd know if we had company. What are you talking about?"

She wore her little stubborn look as she told me, "All I know is, they said the man in white gave them a glass of water, and they were staring over my shoulder like they could see someone. I looked around; I couldn't see anyone but the room's lit up."

I knew that at this time of night, in a mountain storm, no one was going to voluntarily drive up our driveway. It intimidated the most experienced drivers.

Still, we had a rear door, which opened into the back bedrooms. Anyone acquainted with our home could get in without our knowing it. Living this far out in the country, we never locked our doors, but now I became concerned. I wanted to know who was in the bedroom with my young sons.

My father, in the meantime, finished building up the fires and lighting the kerosene lamps. I called to him, "Dad, please go check on the boys."

When he went in to see how his grandsons were, he came back into my room wearing a baffled look. His face, like Vesta's, seemed to radiate light.

"Dad, are my babies all right?"

"Yes, I guess so."

"Are they asleep?"

"No."

"Did you give them a drink of water?"

"They didn't need it."

"But Dad, they asked for water."

"I'm telling you, they didn't need it."

Realizing my father was disturbed, I ignored my labor pains, and asked my father.

"Dad, why don't they need it?"

"When I went into their bedroom, it was lit up brighter than any light bulb, and there's no electricity on in the house."

I could not seem to grasp what Vesta and my father told me. "What do you mean, the room's lit up?"

Impatiently, Dad replied, "I don't know—it was just bright. I noticed the boys had a strange look on their faces. They each held a glass of water in their hands, and I asked them where they'd gotten it. Tootie told me, 'The man in white gave it to us. The man said, "Shhh! Your Mommie is all right, but you're upsetting her with your crying when she can't come to you. Be good now, and be quiet and soon you will have a baby sister. In the morning you can see your

Mommie and your new baby sister.""

When Dad gave me the same information my little sister did, I realized their guardian angel had come to comfort two frightened little boys. I relaxed, and concentrated on having the new baby. Mom delivered my baby daughter. This created a special bond between Mom and her granddaughter, Gloria Jean.

When Dr. Jean arrived, Vesta was sitting on the couch in the front room holding her precious, little niece, and Dr. Jean commented, "Well, I can see that things are pretty well under control here."

It is wonderful to know God takes time to comfort the little ones when we are not able to.

He is ever on watch.

***

Vesta's big complaint today is she did not get to see the angel. She knew the boys saw someone, but when she looked in the direction they were looking, she did not see anyone. However, she knew the room was lit in an unnatural light. Dr. Jean arrived one-half hour after my baby was born. The nurse, for some strange reason, failed to deliver any of my mother's messages. My husband, Harold, and my brother, Everett, ended up in a ditch driving on unfamiliar roads in a rainstorm. The Model A had poor headlights, and at night in a rainstorm, it was hard for them to see where they were going. They had a difficult time getting the car out of the ditch and back on the road. Since Dr. Jean had a newer car with better headlights, they decided to follow her car home to the ranch.

LARRY AND GOD

WHEN VESTA, MY SEVENTEEN-YEAR-OLD SISTER, and I realized there would be an old-fashioned camp meeting in Lodi, not far from the city of Sacramento where we lived, we were intrigued. Our mother wrote she would be attending the meetings, and living in a tent with her sister, Aunt Beula. She thought it would be nice if we joined her. It would be a great opportunity to visit with our relatives. We knew all the great aunts and our grandmother would be attending. It would be like a family reunion, and we were brought up to obey and respect our great aunts and great uncles, as well as love them.

Early Sabbath morning, Vesta, who spent the summer with me, helped get my three children ready for the trip. Hal was eight, Larry six, and Jeanie was four years old. After we loaded the car with food for our lunch, we drove to Lodi. The children chattered in the back seat of my 1939 Chevrolet, as Vesta and I planned our day.

"Vesta, we'll take Hal to the junior tent, Larry to the primary tent, and Jeanie to the kindergarten. Are you going to the adult tent with me, or the youth tent?"

"I think I'll go to the youth."

"Okay. Whoever gets out of our meeting first, will gather the children up, and we'll meet at the youth tent. With this many people attending, we have to have some place to meet."

"That sounds like a good idea."

As we walked from tent to tent, making sure my children were in the right place, we met several of the greats. It was wonderful, meeting so many family members you only saw occasionally. A nice warm feeling filled my soul, as each great-aunt greeted us with a warm smile. They remarked on how happy they were to see us.

My meeting lasted longer than I planned and I was beginning to worry about whether the children would find Vesta. When I arrived at the kindergarten tent, it was empty.

The primary and junior tents were also empty. Hurrying to where the youth were meeting, I hoped my children had managed to find Vesta.

When I neared there, over the loud speaker, I heard Elder Freeman giving an altar call. But instead of quietness, ripples of laughter greeted me. This amazed me, as Elder Freeman was a charismatic preacher and the young people loved him. He urged them to seriously think about their future, and maybe tonight would be the last chance they had to surrender their hearts to God.

It shocked me when I heard loud guffaws. My mind started asking, 'What is going on here?' As the minister struggled on with his appeal, the laughter grew louder. Stepping inside the tent, my eyes searched for Vesta and my three little Smedleys. I spotted Vesta and Hal, slunk down as low in their seats as they could get. Jeanie looked mesmerized as she stared toward the platform. As Elder Freeman manfully continued to try to convince the young people and give his altar call, the laughter became louder.

I became frantic, as I searched for my missing little boy, but I did not spot him anywhere. When my eyes moved to the platform where the minister was still trying to win souls for God, my mind refused to accept what I was seeing. I was mortified. Larry was up on the platform behind the minister, aping him in all his movements. He moved in concert with Elder Freeman, and when he shook his finger, Larry shook his finger; when he raised his arms up to heaven, Larry did the same.

Glancing over where Vesta was sitting with my other two offspring, I became furious. *Why didn't she go and take him off the platform?* I wondered, but it was obvious she had no intention of being identified with her nephew's behavior. This was one unwelcome task I was forced to do myself.

Running around the outside to the back of the tent, I climbed the stairs to the platform where the ministers were sitting. It amazed me none of them looked at Larry; he stood right next to them. Instead, they all sat up straight, staring straight ahead, and acting like they preferred being somewhere else. I marched out on the stage, took Larry's hand and led him off of the platform and out of the tent. When Vesta saw me on the stage, she stood up, took Hal's and Jeanie's hands and walked out of the tent to wait for me.

I was seething inside. I jumped all over Vesta. "For heaven's sake, why didn't you go up there and stop him from mocking the minister?"

"Do you think I wanted any of my friends to know I was even related to him?"

I couldn't argue with her teenage logic. I was upset that I had to go up there to claim him, letting the world know that he belonged to me. We walked over to our mother's tent. It was growing dark. By the time we got there, the news had already reached them.

Aunt Beula met me with, "I was so ashamed when Mrs. Barker stopped by and told me MY NEPHEW mocked the minister! Do you realize in the Bible when the boys mocked Elisha, the prophet, the bears came out and ate them? I don't want *my* nephew destroyed for mocking a man of God. You must spank him now!"

My anger had subsided by the time I walked to Mom's tent, but I knew Larry needed correcting, so I upended him and paddled him with my bare hand.

Mom quietly said, "I think we need to pray to God and ask for forgiveness for Larry."

So we knelt down and prayed.

We were hardly back up on our feet, when my great-aunt Lulu came charging into the tent. "Mona, is it true? Did Larry really make fun of a minister?"

"Yes, Aunt Lulu."

"He must be punished. Now!"

"I already did."

"This is too serious to just give him a pat and tell him to behave. Spank him now! Do you realize I am one of the founding fathers— err—founding mothers of this campus, and all the ministers know me? After all, I just returned from being a missionary, and can you imagine how I felt when someone came up to me, and asked if he was related to ME? And I had to confess he was? SPANK HIM!"

In face of her determination I felt sick, but obediently turned Larry over my knee again and paddled his little rear end.

"Mona, we must pray for his soul."

This was easier on me to pray again for Larry, than to spank him, so we knelt down and everyone prayed for Larry's soul again.

The poor little boy was quietly sobbing each time another great-aunt came storming into the tent. The next one to arrive was Aunt Ruby. She huffed and puffed as she arrived. "Emily, I just heard the horrible news. It's all over the campus that YOUR grandson was mocking a man of God. You must punish him."

Mom quietly said, "We already spanked him twice, and have prayed twice with him."

"Well, I can't face my friends knowing MY great-great-nephew was making fun of a minister. You have to spank him so I can tell my friends I personally saw him punished."

I glanced at Mom, but she was brought up to obey her aunts, and she just gave me a sympathetic look. I spanked Larry again. Aunt Ruby demanded we pray with him again. We did.

When the next great-aunt arrived, I started feeling rebellious over their demanding Larry be punished. Great-aunt Bessie was worried. "Do you realize he can be lost, and not go to heaven?"

Mom said, "Aunt Bessie, we already spanked him three times, and have prayed with him three times. I think that should be enough."

"I'll concede he may not need spanking again, but I want to pray for his soul."

Down on our knees on the hard ground we knelt.

When great-aunt Irene arrived, she just looked sad. "I could hardly believe it was Larry. I feel shocked. May we kneel down and pray for him?"

Obediently all the aunts, Mom, Vesta, the children and I knelt down for one more prayer. By this time, Vesta was beginning to get tired, and she leaned over and whispered, "We better get out of here before Grandma shows up!"

I thought that was a good idea, but before we could get away, Aunt Bernice showed up gasping for breath. "Emily, I just heard the news that my favorite little nephew is in danger of going to hell. After all, he was named after my son, and we must pray for him!"

You can't argue with saints who want to pray, so once more we knelt. The tent seemed to shrink as each great-aunt arrived.

Vesta whispered, "Let's get out of here," but it was too late. As I tried to gather my three children up and leave the crowded tent, Great-Aunt Rose arrived. The sisters all started talking. I refused to spank him again. The great aunts then announced, "You must take him and make him apologize to Elder Freeman."

We started out with Larry holding my hand, his eyes downcast. A little hiccup of a sob escaped him. We couldn't find Elder Freeman. A man, with a devilish gleam in his eye, told me, "Poor man. He couldn't take it, and he left the campus feeling a total failure," His lips twitched where a grin was striving to escape.

The great aunts decided Larry had to apologize to some minister before he could be free of his disgrace.

It was suggested we go to the tent next to us, where Elder Sage, our own minister, was living. Larry reached up and patiently took my hand and we went next door. The tent flap had been open, but I could see them quickly tying it from the inside. We heard low voices coming from the tent before I went over, but when I quietly said, "Knock knock," there was complete silence as if those inside were holding their breath. Again I repeated, "Knock knock," but there was no answer.

When I went back to Mom's tent, Aunt Beula lowered her voice as she commented to me, "I don't blame Elder Sage. He doesn't want any part of this fiasco. This is ridiculous how the aunts are behaving. I'm sorry I insisted Larry be punished."

The great aunts next decided I must find any minister and have Larry confess his misdeeds to him. Vesta looked at me with sympathy, but also a look of, *I'm sure glad I'm not involved.*

Hal and Jeanie sat on the bed like they were afraid to move for fear their great-aunts might take notice of them and decide they needed spanking just for good measure. Larry and I walked hand in hand until I found a minister. Larry's eyes were swollen from crying. When I told the minister the story, he asked, "Have you prayed with him?"

"Yes, sir. Seven times. And he's been spanked three times because my great aunts demanded it."

"My word, child. You go back and tell those great aunts of yours to mind their own business and not interfere with the way you're raising your child. They have insisted on his being over-punished. What you should have done was ask him why he did it, explained why it was wrong, and told him not to do it again. "Why did you do that, son? What were you thinking?""

Larry looked up at the minister and said softly, "It just felt right. I think that's what I'm supposed to do with my life."

***

This took place in 1950 when parents still spanked their children. We were taught in church, "Do not spare the rod and spoil the child." This was not considered child abuse in 1950.

My biggest regret is not immediately asking Larry why he was imitating the minister. This would have spiked the great-aunts demand for punishment. Larry grew up and became a minister, and later entered the army as a chaplain. He recently retired from the Army as a colonel, and now is preaching in a small church in Georgia.

GOD'S VOICE

I THOUGHT I HAD A STABLE, happy marriage. My husband, Harold, seemed loving and contented at home. We had three wonderful children, and he was attentive and helpful around the house. My neighbor told me she was envious of our wonderful relationship, as my husband was never late coming home from work.

When I had two strange dreams, I told my husband about them. In my dreams, I saw a young, attractive woman. She appeared to be working at the motor pool where my husband worked. In my dreams, Harold and this young woman were having an affair. When I woke up crying, I told him about this unsettling dream, and Harold asked me what she looked like. When I described her, in a quiet voice he commented, "I wonder why you dreamt that?"

Again I dreamt he was having an affair. This girl was so clear in my dream that I knew if I ever saw her I would recognize her. I woke up crying after each dream. However, after being held in Harold's arms, with him assuring me he loved me, I felt reassured this was a nightmare.

Shortly after these dreams, I was awakened by a loud man's voice I thought was God, calling my name. I sat straight up in bed, and answered, "What, God?"

The thought crossed my mind; this is the way he called Samuel as a small child. The strong voice was very clear, as he said, "God wants you to know."

I immediately answered, "What, God? What?" But there was no more conversation.

I pleaded, "What, God? What do you want me to know?" No answer. I sat up in bed for a long time, wondering about this strange conversation. The next morning I discovered what God wanted me to know. My husband and I were laughing, and my husband asked me to get his wallet, and take out a phone number he needed. I got his wallet, and as I opened it, out fell a folded postcard. I started reading it, and as Harold realized what I had in my hand, he made a dash across the room to get it. He was too late. In one paragraph, my life was irrevocably changed!

A woman was describing taking a shower with my husband, and how when I thought he was deer hunting, he was at her apartment. She went on, "Please plan another deer trip next weekend so we can shower together again. Love, Joanne."

His friend had driven to our house on Friday afternoon, and picked him up for their deer hunting trip. He gave me a sweet, loving goodbye kiss and I stood there and waved until he was out of sight. Sunday night, they brought him home, and he told me they never saw a deer.

I realized my husband was having an affair with his new secretary. She was eighteen years old. Her husband was a chaplain's assistant in the army, and was stationed in Japan. Her husband planned on being a minister, but in his church this became impossible after they divorced. My husband bought new clothes to keep at her apartment. When I finally met her, I recognized my husband's new secretary was the girl in my dreams. I was devastated.

I was the leader of the kindergarten division in my church, and held this position for five years. After crying for several days, I telephoned the church and asked to have my pastor come see me. I told the secretary my husband and I were separated, and I needed counseling and prayers, as my husband did not want a divorce, but he was infatuated and having an affair with a young girl half his age.

No one came. Several more days passed, as I wept heartbrokenly, and I telephoned the pastor's secretary again, pleading I needed someone to come and counsel and pray with me.

Two elders of the church came. I didn't really feel any comfort after they prayed, and when they got up to leave, I still felt empty. In the process of leaving, they propositioned me, one insinuating that he understood the "certain needs" of divorcees, and would happily take care of them.

The other one, with his Bible under his arm told me, if I would date him, he would divorce his wife. He went on to tell me he had been in love with me for years and wanted to marry me. I should have telephoned the pastor and told him about their conduct, but I was in no condition to think logically. I was shocked at their conduct; I stood there speechless, staring at both of them. I felt abandoned by my husband, and now by God. In my despair, I felt, *if this is what church is all about, why bother?* I wanted nothing to do with this kind of 'Christianity.' I knew that I could not worship God with these two men on the platform. I quit going to church.

I insisted my children continue to go to church and drove them there. When church was out, I returned to pick them up. No one came from church to find out why I no longer showed up to lead the kindergarten department and attend church. It was as if I had never been a member.

Becoming a single mother with three teenage children was difficult. My parents and family were very supportive, and they offered to have me move back home to the ranch, but I felt my children needed the stability of their own home.

It became particularly hard when Harold failed to pay child support for over a year. He paid it faithfully until he married Joanne, and she took over handling his money. Then the child support stopped. After a year of struggling, I hired a lawyer and the child support was reinstated.

I dated various men for several years, and my three teenagers took delight in scaring off the men they didn't like. When I came out dressed up to go out on a date, the three sat with innocent looks on their face.

"Where's Paul?"

"I don't know, Mom—he just jumped up and said he forgot something."

This happened several times before I wised up that this was their way of getting rid of a prospective stepfather they didn't like. Today they enjoy reminiscing about how they "inspected my dates and removed the ones who failed their tests."

Some of the blind dates my friends and family arranged for me were obnoxious, so I refused to go on another blind date. My two girlfriends, Connie and Vi, were determined they arrange a date with a man named Jack, and I was just as determined I would not meet him. When they sang his praises, I came back with, "If he is so wonderful, why don't you date him?"

Connie told me, "I did, Mona, but it was like being with a big brother. No chemistry. We never even kissed. But he is wonderful."

Vi gave me the same answer.

After a year of hearing how wonderful this man was, and just so perfect for me, I was sick of hearing his praises sung and the sound of his name. I told them, "I'll never date another blind date, so drop it please."

One day, the three of us were eating in an Italian restaurant, when a very handsome man walked in. He was well over six feet tall, lean and broad shouldered. His curly, blonde hair was attractive, and his large, blue eyes were beautiful. He walked with the air of a self-confident man.

My heart gave a leap, and I leaned forward and whispered, "Why doesn't anyone ever introduce me to a man like that?" I put my hand to my chest and dramatically said, "Be still, my heart!"

At that moment he waved at the girls, called, "Hi, Connie and Vi," and kept moving across the restaurant. The girls broke into giggles, and then dissolved into laughter until tears were running down their faces. I indignantly asked them, "Just what did I say that is so funny?"

In unison, the girls gasped between laughing, "That's Jack."

I sat there dumbfounded. I looked over my shoulder and thought, "To think I kept refusing to meet him."

After our introduction, when Jack came home to meet my children, they loved him right away. Jack taught my sons how to hunt, and gave them their first rifle. He taught Jeanie how to fish, and he complained she caught more fish than he did. Jack took his speedboat out to Lake Tahoe, and taught us how to water-ski. He gave my sons their first flying lessons in his airplane, and taught my sons how to drive a car. He also showed the boys how to cut trees down and saw up the firewood on a ranch he owned. He spent more time with my children than their father. Life became so much happier after I met the man who fulfilled all of my dreams.

Jack and I married, and I realized God knew what was best for me. It just took a while before I realized I should never have quit going to church while I was grieving over a failed marriage. I feel blessed with the marriage God had waiting for me.

THE SUICIDAL MAN

ONE SPRING DAY with my front door open to catch the warm breeze, I ironed my children's clothes. While enjoying the soft music on my radio, I thought I heard a cry for help. Turning off the radio I heard, "Help!" Straining my ears trying to determine which direction it came from, I thought the cry had grown fainter. I decided to investigate.

Several people were gathered near the porch of my girlfriend, Connie. When his faint cry for help reached me again, I ran down to her house to see who was in trouble. A man, lying on Connie's steps, pleaded for help. I didn't know him, but he looked like he might be one of the neighbors who lived across the street.

What a gruesome sight— blood splattered across the sidewalk and pools of blood were beginning to congeal on her steps where he had collapsed. The sight of so much blood made me feel ill. Looking down at him, I saw both of his wrists were cut and bleeding. Connie and the other neighbors were standing there, watching him bleed to death! Connie, only nineteen, became frightened when she came to her door and found a strange man bleeding on her doorsteps.

Taking a wrist in each hand, I started pressing on them to stop the bleeding. I ordered, "Connie, bring me gauze and tape."

When I started issuing orders, Connie ran to supply me with the needed articles.

In a soothing tone of voice, I told him, "I'm taking you to the hospital," while I taped each wrist.

He could not stand by himself, and I found it impossible to lift him. I recognized four of the men standing in the crowd. Taking charge again, I said, "Tony, get over here and help me put him in my car."

Once he was in my car, the neighbor pleaded, "Please don't take me to the emergency hospital! It's against the law to attempt suicide, and they'll lock me up. Please don't take me there! I did change my mind."

I didn't know what to do. The man needed medical help, but I also knew he would be locked up in the mental hospital.

His husky voice pleaded with me, "I don't want to die. I had a horrible fight with my wife, and when she left to go to church, I decided to end it all. After looking in the mirror with the blood streaming into the washbasin, I changed my mind, and came over here looking for help."

His voice broke. "I thought I was going to die. No one would help me. I collapsed on her steps, and couldn't climb them to ring the doorbell. I started calling for help and the people just gathered around and watched me bleed. You're the only one willing to help me. Please don't take me to the hospital. They arrest people who try to commit suicide."

His pleading put me in a quandary. He needed more help than I could give him, and I wondered if I would be an accessory to a crime if I didn't take him to the emergency room. My mind kept saying over and over, *What am I going to do with him? What am I going to do? He needs more help than I can give him.*

His soft pleading began to wear me down as I drove. "Please, I'll never do it again. I don't want to die."

After driving for a few minutes, he changed his tactics. "Will you take me to my sister's?"

He needed emergency care, but after his tearful persuasion, I agreed. I decided I would leave it up to his family as to whether he needed psychiatric help. He gave me directions to his sister's home. When we arrived and she came to her door, she gave me a suspicious look.

When I told her, "I have your brother in my car because he attempted suicide, and cut his wrists," shock spread across her face. With a bewildered look, she stood as still as a statue, looking at my car and her brother. I began to wonder if he was mistaken in thinking she would help him. With her screen door between us, she continued standing there, as if she couldn't believe what she was hearing.

"He doesn't want to go to the emergency room, and asked me to bring him here. He told me you loved him. I need you to help me, as he is too weak from loss of blood to walk by himself."

When I commented, "He said you loved him," this broke the spell. She shoved the screen door open so quickly that it hit me in the face as she ran to her brother. She opened the car door to help him out, but realized it would take both of us holding him to get him into her house. After we managed to move him into her home, I stayed for another twenty minutes, and when I felt comfortable he wasn't going to die, I drove home.

I moved away, and often wondered what happened to him.

***

Years later, while driving down a seldom traveled country lane, my tire went flat. This upset and worried me, as I knew changing the tire on a curve could be dangerous. I hastily prayed to God to help me change the tire and keep me safe. A car drew up behind me, and parked in such a manner, it protected my car. A smiling young man got out and without saying a word to me, took the lug wrench from my hand and started changing my tire. I was stunned, but grateful for this stranger's helpfulness.

An older man got out of the car, and walked toward me. "Do you remember me?"

"No, I'm sorry I don't."

He smiled, "You saved my life, and I always wanted to do something for you to show my appreciation. I didn't know how to get in touch with you. I'm the suicidal man whose life you saved years ago."

His son, while changing the tire, looked up at my astonished face and said, "I want to thank you for giving me my father! I can't imagine what my life would have been like without him. When you passed us, Dad said, 'There's the lady who saved my life,' so I stepped on the gas, and prayed we could catch you. We both wanted to do something for you, and let you know how much it meant to us, so we prayed God would stop your car. And He did!"

The older man said, "I've given my heart to God, but if I had died that terrible day from committing suicide, I would have been lost. I'm so grateful I'm alive, and able to love and follow Jesus, and now I finally have the chance to show my appreciation. You were the only one willing to help a stranger."

I never imagined God using a flat tire to answer someone's prayer.

18

THE LORD'S PRAYER

MY BROTHER, NORM, and his wife, Dede, were gracious enough to allow Jack and I to get married in their backyard. Elder Ernest Mansell and his wife, Edith, sent word to me that Elder Mansell would not be able to perform the marriage, because Jack was not an Adventist, but wild horses could not keep them away from our wedding, because they thought so much of Jack, and they loved me.

We had a simple wedding, with just family members attending. Norm and Dede's little girl, Debby Dee, four years old, was our flower girl, Norm was Jack's best man, and Vesta was my maid of Honor, with my three children taking part. Jeanie handled the guest book, and Harold and Larry help seat the family. I asked my brother, Elton Adams, to sing the Lord's Prayer while we were still kneeling. I had no idea what the result from that simple request would be for twenty-five years.

One day, while attending the Carmichael SDA church in Sacramento, I went to the rest room during the intermission. There was a long line of women waiting to use the restroom, and since I am a people watcher, and listen to other conversations, I was enjoying the wait.

A lady came in, and exclaimed with happiness at seeing another lady, she had known many years ago. The conversation went something like this:

"I am delighted to see you, Sally. In fact, I am thrilled. Do you mind if I ask you a question?"

"Not at all. It is good to see you, also."

"When did you come back to God? I know the last time I saw you, you were out of the church, and you were bitter and seemed determined never to come back."

Laughing, she responded, "I don't mind telling you. It was a strange experience, and definitely God speaking to me and to others. I was running around as usual, doing many things on Sabbath, getting ready for a party that night. I drove over to the Arden Shopping Mall, as I needed some things from the store, and I was in my usual hurry, as I had to get some things for my party. It was just about sundown, on August 1st.

As I climbed out of my car, and locked it, I started rushing to the store, along with other shoppers. The sun was almost set, when over the air, it seemed to come from heaven itself, I heard the Lord's Prayer being sung by a man. It jolted me. I stopped to listen, and looked around, but there was no one anywhere near me singing, other shoppers stopped also, and we all looked at each other, and no one went on into the store.

People coming out of the mall stopped and looked around, also. We all just listened to this heavenly voice as it sang. I got goose bumps on my body, and I knew God was telling me, 'You have no business shopping on my Holy Day.' I quietly answered, 'Yes, Lord,' and went back to my car, climbed in and drove home, determined to always keep Sabbath. I noticed other shoppers turning around and going back to their car, empty handed also. Others looked very thoughtful. I have no idea where the voice came from, but I do know God had that song sung, so that I would come back to him. I have always been careful of Sabbath ever since."

I wanted to tell her it was my brothers beautiful voice singing at my wedding, but God impressed me to keep quiet. God used my wedding to Jack to redeem a lost soul.

"And all thy children shall be taught of the Lord; and great shall be the peace of thy children."
Isaiah 54:13

JEANIE

WHEN JEANIE WAS SIXTEEN, she decided she wanted to go boarding school with her brother, Larry. Soon, she joined a prayer band and started praying for her father and grandfather. My father loved visiting Milo Academy, and on one of his trips to visit his granddaughter, a young girl was introduced to my father as 'Grandpa West.' She greeted him with, "Oh, you're Grandpa West—I've been praying for you."

After meeting several other girls who told him this also, he felt so impressed with young girls' praying for an old man they didn't know, he stopped smoking and secretly started Bible studies with the minister. One day when he was about seventy years old, he telephoned each of his seven living children with; "I want you in church in Lodi at 4 P.M. next Sabbath. Goodbye," and he hung up.

The telephone lines flew from Fort Bragg, Ukiah, Bakersfield, Sacramento and Fair Oaks as we telephoned each other and asked, "Do you have any idea why Dad has given us all the command to drive to Lodi next week?" Dad lived in Placerville, but my mother was in Lodi taking care of her mother. We were baffled, especially my brother, Bill, who didn't go to church. But even at our age, when our father told us to do something, we did it.

When Sabbath arrived, we were all faithfully sitting in the front of the church, wondering what it was all about. When the curtain was pulled aside and we saw our brother-in-law, Elder Donald Mansell in the baptismal fountain, and my father walking down into the pool to be baptized, we were all happily surprised. Dad had kept his secret and really had us all thrilled. When Dad came out of the pool and was ready for our hugs and kisses of joy, he told me, "Now I too have the blessed hope of seeing my son, Henry, and my precious mother." I never had thought of the heartache Dad was going through when we all talked about seeing Henry in heaven, and he would be quiet, knowing he was not following God.

This wonderful event was because Jeanie had asked for prayers for her grandfather, and some teenage girls were praying for a "Grandpa" they didn't know, and it impressed him so much, he took Bible studies.

One day I received a telephone call that all parents dread. Mrs. Russell, the nurse at Milo Academy, called us to tell us the Jeanie had suffered a blow to the head, and she had quit breathing three times in the ambulance on the way to the hospital, and Mrs. Russell had to give her mouth-to-mouth resuscitation.

Dr. Fox later telephoned us to tell us he didn't expect her to live; she was unconscious, and had a blood clot on the brain. He did not want us to drive to Oregon; he wanted us where the police could notify us when she passed away. I asked if she had any chance to live, and he told me it rested in the hands of God, and the best thing we could do would be to stay home and pray instead of driving, as he was afraid we might be in a wreck, driving under those circumstances.

He was emphatic—we must stay home. This was so hard to do, as we wanted to immediately rush to her side. My husband and I felt like Jacob did. We wrestled with God all night in prayer for her life. We claimed the promise from Hebrews 4:16, "Let us come boldly unto the throne of grace that we may obtain mercy and find grace to help in time of need." After Jack finally went to bed around three A.M., I continued to pace the floor, kneel and pray. I stayed up all night praying for the life of my young daughter.

At eight the next morning, the telephone rang. I was afraid to pick it up, and afraid not to. I desperately sent one more prayer to God, and then answered the phone. Dr. Fox's voice came over the line with a triumphant, "She will live!"

With a feeling of relief flooding my heart, all I could say was, "Thank you God, for your mercy and your love."

DANNY

WE MOVED FROM A LARGE CITY in California to O'Brien, Oregon, where my husband, Jack, went into real estate in the neighboring town of Cave Junction.

The little country church I attended immediately elected me leader of our young people. With all the parents cooperating, I organized and directed the activities of the entire youth program, consisting of children of varied ages. The most challenging part became keeping the teenagers interested. Our head Deacon, Dan, helped me with the young people. He realized my meetings helped to keep the youth occupied on weekends.

Jack didn't go to church at this time, but the ladies in the church told me they prayed for him. One day, Hazel, our head Elder's wife, told me, "Mona, Jack has to eat even if he is working, and since his office is so close to church, please tell him he's invited to our pot lucks; we'll call his office when we have it ready to eat. He can walk over and after lunch he can go back to work."

She never suggested he come to church. The dear ladies asked me about his favorite foods and vied with each other to see if Jack ate their food.

After several months of his enjoying their food, Jack told me, "Honey, I feel guilty about always eating and running. I think I should come to church once in a while just to keep the ladies happy."

When Jack started coming to church regularly, Herb, our Head Elder, suggested Jack take Bible studies. Jack agreed, and Herb drove out to our house every week. Jack enjoyed his Bible studies, and seeing him beginning to accept God made me happy.

One day, I received a telephone call from Miriam, Dan's wife, pleading with me to find her son, Danny. After an argument with his father, he ran away. I asked my daughter, Jeanie, "Do you have any idea where Danny might have gone?"

"Mom, I know one of the places the kids at high school talk about, but I've never been there. I think I can find it."

We drove to Cave Junction and finally spotted Danny. When I pulled up in my car, he gave me a sheepish grin. I quietly said, "Get in the car, Danny. I've come to take you home."

Without a word, he climbed in. I took him to my house and called his mother. She told me, "His father is still angry. Don't bring him now! I'll phone you when Danny can come home."

"Miriam, I don't have an extra bedroom. When Larry went into the Army, I moved LaurieAnne's crib into Larry's bedroom."

"Please, Mona-- let him sleep on the floor."

Heaving a sigh, I agreed to his sleeping on my sofa in the front room. Three days later, she called and said, "Dan's sorry he ran Danny off. You can bring him home now."

The next time I received her frantic phone call she told me, "Mona, please go and find Danny. His father lost his temper out at the barn, and ripped Danny's shirt in their tussle, then took a board and chased him off the ranch. I really have no idea where he is, but I think he's staying at a ranch where they drink and use drugs. Please go and find him and take him home with you. Dan said he can never live at home again, and it's breaking my heart!"

"Miriam, we have two daughters, and no place to put Danny."

She pleaded, "Just put him anywhere. Please give him a home. I love him so much, and he can't ever come home to live."

"I just don't see how I can."

"Mona, he's only fifteen. He has no place to live!"

"I'll talk to Jack and see how he feels." I figured Jack would say no.

What I didn't know was that Dan drove from his ranch into town to Jack's office and pleaded with him to find Danny, and give him a home. Jack, talking to an important client, asked Dan to please sit down until he finished his business, but Dan refused to leave. He demanded Jack's attention now, and told my husband that he wanted him to give his son a home. Jack explained our bedroom situation at home. Dan told him, "You can always remodel and add another bedroom."

Jack felt it took a lot of nerve for Dan to tell him to build his son a bedroom. I agreed with him, but we both also felt sorry for Danny. We held a family conference, talked it over with Jeanie, and asked her how she felt about having her bedroom made smaller. After discussion, we decided for Danny's sake, to remodel the upstairs.

Jack and I drove to the Lonesome Ranch and they invited us in. I saw at a glance why his mother did not want Danny in this environment. Danny stood up when he saw me. He never quibbled. He told his friends goodbye, and walked out the door to our car.

On the way home, I explained, "Danny, we'll make you a bedroom, but until we do, you'll have to sleep downstairs on the sofa."

Danny thanked us for giving him a place to live. His parents never sent any of his clothing. We bought him a complete wardrobe of clothes. During the next year, his grades went up from D's and C's to B's and A's. We felt proud of him. He attended church with us, and instead of sitting with us, he always sat with his mother. His father ignored him.

We kept a fishing boat moored on the coast, and Jack taught him how to fish for salmon. When we went on trips in the airplane, I moved to the back seat with Jeanie and LaurieAnne, and Danny sat in the front with Jack. Once in the air, Jack turned the flying over to Danny. Jack enjoyed having a redheaded teenager in the house. This didn't surprise me, as I felt he missed Larry.

We consulted Children's Services on a regular basis on how to handle certain situations. The Children Services rep told us Dan reported Danny as a runaway each time he ran him off the ranch. He felt Dan seemed determined to send Danny to the reform school, and told us he felt better knowing Danny now lived with us.

One evening when Jack came home from work, he told me, "Dan came into my office. He didn't ask if he could fly my Cessna, he just demanded, 'Jack, I want the keys to your plane.'"

"What did you say? You didn't give them to him, did you?"

"No. I'd think twice before I loaned him my car, let alone my plane."

"What made him think you'd just hand over your keys?"

"I have no idea."

"Have you ever taken him for a ride, or ever given him the idea you'd loan him your new airplane?"

"No. That's why it stunned me. I couldn't think of what to say, so I asked him if he had a current pilot's license. He said he did. I next asked him when the last time he flew a Cessna 172 was, and he said, '5 years ago.' I told him I could take him out Sunday and check him out. He demanded I take him today. I was right in the middle of closing a real estate deal, and told him I didn't have time to check him out today. He demanded my keys anyway, and I told him I'd be remiss as a pilot if I allowed him to fly without first checking him out. When I refused to leave my client, he stormed out of the office. He was so angry, he was red in the face, and the veins were standing out in his forehead. I'm afraid he's going to cause trouble."

"Oh, honey, I'm so sorry. I remember Miriam telling me Dan came in too fast, and crashed his own plane about five years ago. That took a lot of nerve to expect you to just hand over your keys."

"He must have heard I let the Lucas brothers from the lumber company fly my plane, when they needed to see how close the forest fire was to their stand of timber. I checked them out thoroughly before I gave them permission to fly it."

"That was an emergency! You just don't let anyone fly a new airplane!"

"They told me in the office I made an enemy, and when Dan can't have his way, he resorts to doing something to get even."

We wondered what Dan might do, and we soon found out.

Sunday when I answered a knock on my door, our local deputy sheriff stood there with a smirk on his face. He told me, "I've come for Danny."

"Why? Danny hasn't been in any trouble. He's home with us every day after school."

"I'm taking Danny home."

This surprised me. Miriam knew I brought Danny home the other two occasions, after she asked me to find him.

When the deputy next told me, "Mona, you're being charged with contributing to the delinquency of a minor."

This stunned me. I stood there with my mouth open. The deputy looked like he enjoyed seeing my shock and bewilderment. Danny refused to go, and the sheriff dropped his hand to his gun in a threatening manner. I told Danny, "Get in the car. I'll see if I can straighten this out."

He obeyed without question and climbed into the patrol car.

The feeling of betrayal swept over me, and besides feeling hurt, I felt humiliated. The local weekly newspaper published the charges against Jack and me, and we soon received notification when to appear in court. With only five thousand inhabitants in the valley, everyone read the newspaper for any new scandal.

When we arrived in court, Dan, Miriam and Danny sat on one side of the court, the representative from Children's Services on the other, we sat at the end, and the judge faced us.

Dan stood up and ranted about how we stole his son's love from him. We took him fishing, camping, and taught him how to fly, while his other sons worked hard on the ranch. Miriam sat silently, and Dan acted as if we kidnapped Danny. Not once did he mention he asked us to take Danny and give him a home.

The representative from Children's Services stood up and tried to defend us, and the judge told him to shut up, or be in contempt of court. The rep sat back down with a shocked look. He turned to us with sympathy on his face.

Jack tried to tell the judge they asked us to take Danny, but the judge refused to allow either Jack or I to speak, and to keep our mouths shut or be charged with contempt of court. He told us, "If I ever hear you have Danny in your home, I'll throw you in jail. You can never speak to him again, and if you see him walking down the street, you are to cross the street. If you're in a store and he comes in, you leave immediately."

We felt humiliated, being forced to sit and listen to the diatribe against us by Dan and then by the judge.

Danny jumped up and shouted at the judge, "You're not being fair to the Barnes. My parents begged them to give me a home. Why won't you listen to their side?"

The judge ordered Danny to shut up, but he inherited his father's hot temper, and continued to shout at the judge, "If you insist on this unfair ruling, and make me go home to live, where my father beats me and chases me off the ranch every time he loses his temper, I'll make my parents' life so miserable, they'll be sorry for what they did to the Barnes."

Jack wanted nothing more to do with Dan's type of Christianity, and refused to take any more Bible studies. I cried and stayed home from church; Jeanie walked around like a little, lost girl, asking me, "Does this mean I can't speak to Danny at high school?"

With no transportation, Jeanie missed church unless we drove, and we refused to go. I just studied and read my Bible at home and walked the floor and stared out of the window, in abject misery. The feeling of Dan's betrayal overwhelmed me, and I felt Dan might be the cause of Jack losing his soul.

Jack continued working in this small community, knowing we were found "guilty of contributing to the delinquency of a minor." Jack took a lot of ribbing over the situation, when he went to his club. As Jack was the President of the Chamber of Commerce, it became the talk of the town. Some of the ranchers who were acquainted with Dan, phoned us in sympathy, to let me know they did not believe the charges. Others, who knew how Dan begged us to take Danny, were very sympathetic. The church members tried to rally around me, but this did not console me. I felt betrayed by Miriam and Dan. It hurt, knowing they deliberately smeared our name, leaving people wondering if we allowed him to drink alcohol, or worse yet, indulged in some kind of sexual behavior. Little did we know God would solve this problem in His own way.

***

This same deputy sheriff later asked Jack if I would be his campaign manager for him to become our resident deputy, as he didn't like driving to Grants Pass daily. He told Jack he knew if I campaigned for him, he would win. Jack told him he doubted it, as he knew I was still smarting from his grinning over my being charged with contributing to the delinquency of a minor.

The sheriff told Jack, "I was afraid of that, but you should have seen Mona's face when I told her! She had the funniest expression I have ever seen. I had a hard time to keep from laughing, and besides, I knew no one would believe that about her. We all knew the real story! Tell her I'm sorry I added to her embarrassment." It took me quite a while to forgive him.

LARRY

ONE DAY, AFTER FINISHING DINNER, my husband, Jack, left to go to the Lion's Club, in Cave Junction. I gave our curly-headed toddler, LaurieAnne, a bath and read a bedtime story to her. After listening to her prayers, I put her to bed at seven o'clock. Making myself a hot cup of herbal tea, and settling down in my easy chair for a relaxing evening, I opened the evening newspaper. The first thing that caught my eye was the terrifying news: *Four paratroopers killed, eight injured in the 82nd Airborne Division.*

My eyes skimmed over the sickening details and I became terrified this might be my son Larry's outfit. I ran to the bedroom and retrieved one of his letters to compare his address with the outfit where the soldiers were killed. My heart dropped. The company and regiment were the same. Every last detail of his address was the same as the four who were killed.

I didn't know where to turn and couldn't talk to my husband, who was still at the Lion's Club, so, running to the telephone, I placed a person-to-person telephone call to my son in Fort Bragg, North

Carolina. We lived in a tiny community where one man owned the entire telephone company, and the operator knew each of us.

The operator tried repeatedly to place the telephone call, but the line stayed busy. After five minutes, Mrs. Abbott told me, "Mona, you go pray, and I'll keep ringing Fort Bragg."

I knew others had probably already read the newspaper before I did, and were wondering if the accident involved Larry. I went in the front room, and wrestled with God in prayer. I felt lost and alone. Living so far out in the country, there were no close neighbors for me to call on for emotional support. I walked the floor and pleaded with God to protect Larry.

After several hours, the telephone rang and I rushed to answer. Mrs. Abbott told me she was ringing my number. When a soldier answered the telephone, she said, "I have a person-to-person telephone call for Larry Smedley."

The soldier answering the phone said, "He ain't here."

"Do you know where I can reach him?"

"No, Ma'am."

"When do you expect him?"

"I don't."

"May I leave a message for him to call his mother?"

"He can't call his mother."

Interrupting the conversation, I said, "I'll talk to this soldier."

He went into a panic. "I can't talk to you. Your name is on his list, and only the Chaplain can talk to you. He's going to be calling you." He slammed the phone down.

I knew what this meant. My son was dead. The telephone operator told me in a soft voice, 'I'm so sorry, Mona. I'm so sorry."

It became hard to breathe, as my heart hurt every time it beat. I walked the floor and pleaded with God to spare my son's life. Each time I prayed, I heard a voice in my ear tell me, "Why are you asking God to spare his life? This accident took place this morning at seven. It is now after seven in the evening. Larry is dead. Accept it."

Then I would hear another whisper in my ear, "I will answer

before you call."

Could this be true? With no memory of ever reading that verse in the Bible,

I wanted to believe, so continued praying.

One voice became insistent, "Your son is dead. Why do you keep pestering God? Accept the fact."

This discouraged me and while crying, I continued to plead with God, "Please spare his life. Please God."

After a while, the bargaining with God started. "If you will spare his life, I will do whatever you want me to do."

My heart hurt so much, I had dry heaves. After pleading and begging with God and promising all kinds of wild things that I would change in my life, I heard God in a soft but firm voice tell me, "Heal my Church."

I knew instantly what God wanted me to do, and answered God, "I never want to see Dan again! He hurt us, he smeared our name, and he told lies about us. I despise him. God, just tell me something else to do, and I'll do it, but please, please spare Larry's life, but don't ask me to talk to Dan."

Again that soft, insistent voice, "Heal my church."

I fell down on the floor and laid my head in my chair, and sobbed. "God, don't ask that of me. I never want to see Dan's face again. Just tell me something else to do, and I'll do it, but please spare Larry's life."

Like a repetitive refrain, came the three words, "Heal my church."

I lay there and sobbed. After several hours, I gave in to God and said, "All right. I'll go to Dan tomorrow and tell him how he hurt Jack, whether Larry is alive or not."

Jack arrived home from the Lion's Club, and saw my tear-stained face. He asked what was wrong, and I handed him the newspaper. He glanced at me, then at the front page, and his face turned white. I explained about the telephone call to Fort Bragg, and how I was told my name was on the list for the Chaplain to phone. My husband gave me an anguished look, and his voice broke as he said, "Larry's dead."

Dropping his head into his hands, his shoulders began to shake. Finally, he jumped up and ran into the bedroom, shutting the door. I stayed in the front room, not able to go to bed, waiting for the Chaplain to call. I felt peaceful after surrendering to God's will. The tight feeling in my chest left, and I could breathe again. My mind felt numb, however, as I thought about facing Dan the next morning.

Although there was peace inside of me, I still walked the floor, thinking of Larry as a toddler holding my hand. Memories started flooding my mind of Larry as a small child kneeling at my knee at night, lisping his prayers. I remembered his rambunctious teenage years, with more schemes then my other children. He had been a delight to raise, and one who kept me on my toes, trying to stay one step ahead of him.

At a quarter to midnight, the telephone rang. My body was weary as I slowly got up to answer the phone, expecting the dreadful news from the chaplain. Instead the operator said, "I have a collect call from Larry Smedley. Will you accept it?"

Sobbing with every breath I took, I said, "Oh, thank you, God. Thank you, God, oh, thank you, God, thank you." I was so overcome with relief and happiness I could not say the simple word yes, but continued to thank God. The operator told me, "Ma'am, just say yes, and you can talk to him."

"Thank you, God. Thank you, thank you, thank you, God."

Next I heard her say, "Sir, I am supposed to hear the word yes, before I allow you to talk, but if she was able, she would say yes, so go ahead, but I am warning you, this is one conversation I am going to listen to."

"Mom, I'm so sorry!" said Larry, urgently. "I'm back in Fort Bragg and have been standing in line for hours, waiting for the use of the phone to let you know I'm alive! Please stop crying! Mom, I'm not hurt, and I'm alive."

I swallowed a few tears, and said, "Thank you, God", before I could speak to my son. "What happened, Larry? I know they reported you dead."

"After I telephoned you to pray for me, we loaded up in a C130 aircraft, and flew south, to Florida. The jumpmaster told us to take our places. I stood up and hooked my parachute to the line over my head. As long as the light stays red at the head of the aircraft, you don't jump. I was on the right side of the plane ready to jump when a captain unhooked his parachute and walked across the aisle to my side and said, 'Larry, trade places with me.'"

"Did you?"

"Mom, you're never supposed to argue with an officer, but I did. I told him I was in the position the manifest showed. We're all a bit superstitious, Mom, and this was the position I've always jumped from. I finally asked him, "Is this an order?" and he replied, "No, Larry, a request."

"So I told him I didn't want to trade places with him, because I was comfortable with the position I had, and he said, 'Just do it this one time. I want to know what it's like to jump out of your side.'

"About this time, the jumpmaster came back and asked us, 'What the hell is going on here? You're supposed to be ready to jump when I turn your light green, and neither of you are in position.'

"I told him the captain wanted to trade places with me, and I told him I didn't want to. I have always jumped from this position.

"Mom, the jumpmaster was unhappy with the captain, but he is a sergeant, so the jumpmaster finally ordered me to trade places. As he went back to the front of the plane, I could hear him grumbling about officers. When the light turned green, I jumped and had a beautiful fall. It was so peaceful floating down to the ground.

"When I landed, I heard a commotion, and when I looked back, I saw several soldiers gathered around in one area, but I gathered my chute and trotted over to the truck for my ride back to Fort Bragg.

"When I got back to camp and walked into my barracks, there were two soldiers emptying my locker. They had most of my belongings packed. I asked, 'Hey! What the heck are you doing to my belongings?'

"The two soldiers turned around, and they looked shocked. One of the soldiers turned white, and started trembling, and the other man stuttered, 'Man, you're dead.'

"They both kept telling me I was dead, and I kept shouting I was not dead, I was alive. They showed me the orders to pack my belongings as fast as possible, before the other troops came back. That was a spooky feeling, seeing papers that said I was dead.

"One of them had the presence of mind to tell me you'd been sent a telegram saying I was dead, and I'd better run over to headquarters and have another telegram sent to you. I'm so sorry, Mom, you've gone through this heartache. I have stood in line for hours, waiting my turn at the payphone, as I guess all the men are trying to reach their parents to tell them they're alive."

"But what happened, Larry? Why did they say you were killed?"

"Mom, before we go up, there is a manifest that shows each position of the soldiers by their name. I was number eight. The soldiers that jumped and were killed were numbers six, seven, eight and nine. This meant when the spotters saw the captain chopped up in pieces, they reported me as being killed.

"The airplane behind us lost elevation and dropped down. When it did, it flew into the men jumping from my plane, and it killed four paratroopers, and injured about eight others. Because he jumped in my place, the ground spotters reported it was me. Oh, Mom, I knew the captain. I worked for him when I was off duty. That's why he called me by my first name, instead of my last name. We were friends. I mowed his lawn, and I baby-sat for him. He didn't trust everyone with those babies, and he trusted me. He had two toddlers, Mom, and now those babies don't have a daddy anymore!"

Larry's voice choked with emotion. He sounded as if he were crying. My heart ached for the men killed, and their wives and children, but also overflowed with happiness knowing God spared me the heartache of losing my beloved son.

The next day, our grinning deputy sheriff came to my door to show me the two telegrams. One announcing my son's death, and the other one saying he was alive. He refused to give them to me.

"But, George, they are addressed to me," I protested.

"Mona, you have your son back alive—I have the telegrams," he smiled. "I'm going to frame them and hang them on my wall. You can come to the office and read them anytime you want, but I feel I deserve to keep them, 'cause I spared you the agony of believing your son was dead.

"I also felt I owed you one more night's peace of mind, after that stupid stunt I pulled when I came to pick up Danny. I thought you knew me well enough to know I was putting on a show, as I thought it was ridiculous and would never really intimidate you by putting my hand on my gun! I thought it was a big joke, since everyone in town knew you were innocent, and knew Dan's temper!

"I just could not deliver that telegram yesterday. I knew I should—but I felt it might be easier for you to handle in the morning.

"You have no idea what a relief it was to the whole town, when that second telegram came through. People were running from store to store shouting, 'Larry's alive. Larry's alive!' You know, for the mischief that kid got into when he was home, we did all love him, and we're still rooting for him! After he joined the army, we felt he belonged to all of us.

"When I received the telegram saying he was dead, I just sat there, sick. I wanted to wait until morning before bringing it to you. The next thing I knew, a lot of the women in town were crying, and praying for him. I hoped they would have sense enough not to phone you or go see you. I was amazed at how fast the information went through town that he was dead—and the news traveled even faster, that he was alive."

"But, George, how did they know? I live ten miles out on a country road, and I never told anyone!"

Grinning, the deputy sheriff said, "Mona, you forget you're on a party line, and there were three other ladies listening to your whole conversation, besides the telephone operator. When the Sarge said he couldn't talk to you—that your name was on the Chaplain's list, I'd estimate in thirty minutes the whole town started praying for Larry and you. Soon I had men in my office asking me if it were true, that Larry had been killed."

I stood in open mouthed wonder. I never dreamt anyone listened to my private conversations.

George went on talking, "When the operator heard Larry's voice, she just opened all the telephone lines and told everyone at the same time! We all knew within five minutes of your hearing Larry's voice that he was alive. Even before I got the second telegram."

George stood there grinning, while I digested the information everyone in town knew the news that my beloved son was alive.

The news that people listened into my conversations amazed me. I moved from Sacramento, California to this small town in Oregon. As a city girl, I never thought about how a small town might find anything I had to say interesting enough to listen in on my conversations. However, I took solace in knowing that when I suffered my deepest despair, a whole valley of women and men were praying Larry's life would be spared.

***

The newspaper carried this story on the front page:

Larry Smedley Jumps With Doomed Chutists

Larry Smedley, son of Mr. And Mrs. Jack Barnes of O'Brien, was participating in the mass parachute jump at Ft. Bragg, North Carolina last Tuesday, when four paratroopers were killed and eight others injured.

The accident occurred when a C130 aircraft apparently lost altitude and its wing struck a group of the descending parachutists who had jumped from another plane.

In a telephone call to his parents Tuesday evening Larry stated that he was uninjured and knew nothing about the tragedy until after his jump was completed, although he had jumped from the same ship.

***

I knew I promised God to go and confront Dan about his actions, and try to heal God's church. It was still hard for me to face Dan. I did not want to ever see Dan again after his false accusations.

When I arrived at their ranch house, his wife, Miriam, answered the door, and quietly said, "Come in. Dan is in the kitchen painting."

Entering the kitchen, I noticed a stool, and sat down on it. Dan completely ignored me, and continued painting. Miriam went and stood in a corner behind me. I knew by her actions, this was strictly between Dan and I.

In a tearful voice, I went over the whole story of Danny and how I felt betrayed, after what had happened yesterday, and how God spared Larry's life, and the promise I made to God to try to heal His church.

Dan continued painting, without saying one word to me. He listened without interrupting me, then turned to me and in an anguished voice said, "You think life has been hard for you? In public, Miriam has been the dutiful wife, supporting me all the way, but at home, she has made my life miserable. Everyone in town knows the true story, and how I have repaid your generosity. I feel like a heel! I have regretted my actions ever since we left the courthouse. I repaid your friendship in a spiteful manner. Now I am too ashamed to go to church. My wife is angry with me, and my children are unhappy."

"Dan, I haven't been back to church, either. Laurie wants to go to kindergarten and sing songs, and Jeanie is missing the company of the teenagers, since I have refused to drive her to church, and now Jack won't attend church either."

"Well, Mona, what are we going to do? Our kids need to go to church, but I am too ashamed of what I have done to face anyone."

After sitting quiet for a few moments, I came up with this idea. "Dan, let's skip Sabbath School, where everyone will nail us at intermission. I don't feel like talking to anyone. Let's wait until the 11:00 hour, and walk in at the same moment."

Dan was quiet, and then he said, "This sounds good to me. But how will we know when to meet? Or where?"

'Whoever arrives first, park over under the oak tree and wait. Then we will walk in together. I think I should sit between you and Miriam. That way, after church, no one will be able to have a 'cozy' talk with us. They will know we have forgiven each other."

When Sabbath arrived, I was late arriving at church, and Dan was already parked over under the oak tree, waiting for me. We had all the children walk in front of us. My daughter, Jeanie, held LaurieAnne's hand. They sat in a pew in front of us. The minister had already started to preach when we walked in. Miriam came in first, followed by me, then Dan. The minister's mouth fell open, as he stared at the parade marching down his aisle to the front, where no one else was sitting. He stopped his sermon and announced with a beaming face, "Let's all sing hymn number 249, Praise him, Praise Him!, Our church family has been healed."

By leaving the sanctuary together, we didn't have to explain anything to anyone.

In following God's advice, I gained a brother and a sister. Dan's grandchildren call us Aunt Mona and Uncle Jack. In the last forty years, Dan has been a true brother to us.

Larry went on to college, and studied to be a minister. When he was qualified, he rejoined the army as a chaplain, and once more found himself stationed in the 82nd Airborne Division, where he saw combat in Panama and became highly decorated. He recently retired as a Lt. Colonel. I have been truly blessed for forgiving an injustice.

DAD LEARNS TO PRAY

DAD TELEPHONED ME one Saturday evening and told me that he'd lost his glasses. He asked me if I would come and help find them. I should have gone right away, but I was feeling tired. I told him that if he didn't find the glasses by Sunday afternoon, then we would drive to town and help look for them. We lived about 22 miles from him.

Dad was eighty-one and lived alone. I felt guilty for not going sooner, because he couldn't read without them. Of course, this meant that he couldn't read his Bible. Dad always read his Bible at 8 a.m. and 5 p.m. He felt lost without his glasses.

When my husband jack, and my children, Jackie and LaurieAnne and I arrived, I questioned him as to when the last time he'd worn them? He said, "I was reading my Bible for worship and fell asleep."

I thought, *His glasses must be around his chair*. We searched the entire chair area, even tipping the chair over. We spread out and searched, room by room, but we found nothing. I was starting to feel -helpless, and I said "Dad, we need to pray that we can find them". So we knelt down to pray. We each took a turn praying, but dad didn't. I quietly said, "Dad it's your turn."

In an anguished voice, he said, "I never learned to pray, I have always said the Lord's Prayer, or Now I Lay Me, or your mother prayed for us."

This amazed me. I never realized this! I knew during worship, Dad read the Bible and Mom prayed. "Dad, I'll help you pray. I will say a sentence, and then you say it. You need to be able to talk to Jesus yourself. Jesus wants you to tell him yourself when you need something." So I taught my father how to pray the way I did with my children when they were little.

I said, "Dear Jesus, I have lost my glasses. I can't afford to buy new ones. Please show us were my glasses are." Dad repeated this. "Thank you, Jesus, for finding my glasses for me." Dad again repeated this. Everyone said amen. Dad stood up, and I said quietly, "Dad, see how easy it is to talk to Jesus? Now you can tell him thing every day."

We set out searching for the glasses again, but still no luck. I felt discouraged. I went into Dad's kitchen and opened up the refrigerator door. I got out a dill pickle and started eating it. I quietly talked to my lord. "God, My father needs you to show him that you listen to him and answer his prayers, so that he will be able to talk to you himself when he needs to. Please show me where the glasses are."

Jack walked into the front room and saw me standing there, "Mona, aren't you going to help search for your father's glasses?"

"I am waiting for Jesus to show me where they are." Upon saying that, the glasses flew through the room, and landed at my feet. Dad, Jack, Laurie, and Jackie had the most stunned looks on their faces. I gulped and quietly said, "Here are your glasses, Dad."

Dad and Jack kept trying to figure out how the glasses could have flown through the air and landed at my feet. They finally had to accept the only explanation. It must have been my Guardian angel who found them and threw them to me, so Dad's faith could grow and he would be able to talk to Jesus himself.

I was so thankful for this episode later, as the night he died, I went to see him, and finally got up the courage to talk to Dad about his salvation. He said to me, "I've talked to Jesus, and he has forgiven me for all my sins."

He died two hours later from a heart attack.

23

WHAT GOES AROUND

SHORTLY AFTER JACK and I married, we moved to Fair Oaks, California. When we met our new next-door neighbor, I was delighted. I had previously worked with Jan at McClellan Air Force Base. We eagerly renewed our friendship, and her baby girl captivated me. My children were all teenagers, and I found myself going next door on any pretext to visit Jan, just to hold and rock this cuddly baby to sleep. Nikki was six months old, and her smiles warmed my heart. When she saw me, her eyes would light up with love, and both of her little arms propelled like windmills from excitement.

One Sunday while lying on my front-room couch and totally absorbed in reading my book, without knowing why, I suddenly threw it down and ran to my front door. In my haste I found myself fumbling, trying to unlock the door. As soon as I jerked it open, Jan appeared running up to my door and thrust little Nikki into my arms. The baby looked lifeless; her little legs and arms were dangling and her head drooped backwards. Her face wore a mottled purple cast. Jan was almost incoherent, as she tried to tell me what was wrong. She sobbed, "I was ironing, and Nikki was sitting on the floor near me, looking at a magazine, when I heard her gasping. She had torn a corner off the page and swallowed it. I can't get it out."

After trying to dislodge whatever was blocking her airway with my finger, I realized time was fast running out for Nikki. I flipped her over in my arms, and slapped her back with my hand. The paper came flying out of her mouth. The precious little one gasped as air rushed back into her lungs. Nikki's color improved and she started crying. This was music to my ears, and I wanted to cuddle her after the scare of thinking she might die. However, Nikki glared at me with anger, then turned around and reached for her mother. From that day on, she refused to allow me to rock or hold her. I am not sure if she blamed me for hitting her on her back or for her not being able to breathe.

I still don't know who caused me to throw down a book, and run to my door and unlock it, and reach for the baby. If I had waited for the front doorbell to ring and walked to the door, Nikki would have died. Was it Nikki's guardian angel? Or was it mine that propelled me to my front door?

*** *Four years earlier* ***

We moved to O'Brien, Oregon, and my niece, Terry West, age twelve, spent the summer. Terry kept her nose in a book all during her visit. When we took her to the Deer Park, instead of feeding the animals, she read her book. We took her to the Oregon Caves and she read a book all the way there. The only satisfaction we received was when she couldn't read while walking through the cave. We drove Terry to Grants Pass to watch car races, and she packed a book along to read while we watched the races. We took Terry for a ride up the Rogue River in a jet boat, and with water spraying into her face, she read her book.

We wracked our brains trying to find some entertainment for her, so she could go back to Los Angeles with happy memories of the summer she spent in Oregon. All she wanted to do was read. My niece seemed oblivious to anything we planned for her.

One day, Terry was upstairs lying on her bed and reading a romance book. She kept the radio going full blast. I wished she would turn it down, but she seemed to be going through some teenage rebellion. I decided not to push the issue over the loudness. Terry acted as if it pained her to talk to me. However, she made it plain she wanted to spend the summer with me.

One day, while taking my vitamins, I swallowed three Vitamin E capsules. The pills lodged in my throat, and the water came gushing back up and out of my nose and mouth. My throat was completely blocked, and I was in serious trouble. The capsules were gelatin, so I knew they wouldn't dissolve immediately. With only a few minutes to live if I couldn't dislodge them, I tried patting myself on my back with no luck. Next, I tried hitting myself in the chest, but this didn't work. Running my finger down my throat didn't help, either.

Visions of my husband or Terry finding me lying dead on the floor flashed through my mind.

Just as my eyesight started to fade, Terry hit the floor above my head, and came running. It sounded as if she were taking the steps two at a time. When she arrived at my side, I was still bent over the sink, and she hit my back twice with her fist. The capsules exploded out of my throat.

With tears streaming down my face, I straightened up and turned to Terry and asked her, "How did you know I was choking to death? You had the radio going so loud you couldn't hear me."

With a startled look on her face, Terry answered, "I didn't know. I don't know what happened. I was lying on my bed reading, and the next thing I knew I found myself running across the bedroom floor, and then leaping down the stairs. You were doubled over the sink, and I just hit you hard. I don't know why."

I do. My guardian angel sent her.

***

Whenever I see a baby playing with a magazine or newspaper, I either take it away from her, or tell the mother this story. I get chills when I see a baby playing with paper.

TELL JESUS

I KNEW MY FATHER was going to die. He was eighty-one, with a bad heart and terminal cancer. I just wasn't ready for him to die. I could verbally acknowledge it, but I couldn't accept it in my heart.

Dad had cancer for more than ten years, but each time the doctor who operated held out hope. This time, when the doctor came out of surgery he knelt in front of me, took my hands in his, and told me and my daughter, Jeanie, that Dad had not one but three types of bladder cancer. He stayed kneeling at my feet, as he gently gave me the bad news.

My mind shut down. I couldn't accept or understand what the doctor was saying; it was as if he was speaking in a foreign language.

I asked, "How long does Dad have?"

"Maybe one to two weeks."

My mind rejected this information. He said, "You should pray your father will die from a heart attack, as the type of cancer he has is very painful."

I pleaded with him, "Can't he live longer than one or two weeks?"

He quietly told me, "You shouldn't want your father to live longer. The pain would be too intense."

The next day Dad was in surgery again to stop some internal bleeding. From that, Dad developed a staph infection. After three weeks in isolation he came home. He started cobalt treatments, and I was determined my father would live as long as possible.

I became angry with God about what my father was going through. Outwardly, I appeared to accept it. Inwardly, I was at war with God. I rebelled over God's decision to let my father die. I prayed that God would spare him as long as He could without Dad suffering, but I still wanted my father healed. I knew God could heal him, so I blamed God when He didn't.

I found it hard to go to church with all this anger and resentment boiling inside of me. My mother was in a rest home, bedfast and paralyzed from three major strokes. I drove nearly ninety miles daily to see her, and now my Daddy was dying. Life just did not seem fair.

I reluctantly accompanied my husband, Jack, and our son to church. That Sabbath morning a young doctor got up to sing. Weldon Fletcher has a rich, beautiful voice, and I always looked forward to hearing him sing, but this morning my seething resentment toward God made me unaware of anything around me.

Suddenly, the words and the music of the song became so personal; it seemed as if Dr. Fletcher were singing just to me. I felt as though God had inspired him to sing *Tell Jesus,* with words by John Peterson.

The words, "When the way is dark before you," broke my heart, and I started crying. Dr. Fletcher looked at me with questioning eyes as he sang. I tried to stop the tears, but couldn't. I sobbed all through his song.

When my handkerchief was soggy, Jack slipped me his. He quietly asked, "Do you want to leave?" I shook my head no.

God was talking to me through the words, "Jesus has grace to meet your need." The words and music cleansed my soul from all anger, heartache and resentment. The song helped me accept the fact that my father was dying, and my soul was once more at peace with My Lord and my God.

God gave me one more wonderful year with my father without him suffering. Peace reigned in my soul. I was thankful to be able to take care of my father, and I no longer felt anger or resentment knowing I was going to lose him. The song sung by Dr. Fletcher healed my sick soul when a sermon could not.

***

When the way is dark before you,
And the path is hid from view,
When you grope with steps uncertain,
And you know not what to do.

When your heart is nearly breaking
With a crushing weight of woe,
When you seem alone, forsaken,
By the earthly friends you know,

Tell Jesus, tell Jesus,
He will listen, He will heed,
Tell Jesus, blessed Jesus,
He has grace to meet your need.

-John Peterson-

OUR FAITH IS REWARDED

JACK AND I DECIDED to take LaurieAnne and Jackie for a six-week vacation to Mexico. I read in the newspaper, "Don't travel in Mexico unless you take car parts with you," but I could not conceive why we might need any parts as we were driving a new Toyota station wagon.

With Jackie not in school yet, and Laurie in the third grade, our trip was made possible when her teacher made only one condition on our taking her out of school. She had to keep a diary of everything that happened while we were on the trip.

This proved a little embarrassing for me when I needed to make a pit stop. After I got into the Mexican version of a port-a-pot, I locked the door behind me. No matter how hard I tried to get out, the door stayed locked. I could hear men talking very close to the door, and I started yelling, "Help! Help! Get me out of here."

I heard men chuckle, but no one came to rescue me. I started feeling desperate when they left me in a hot, stinking, little roadside toilet. I began to think I might faint from the smell and heat. Jack decided to come and investigate what took so long. He heard me banging on the door and yelling for help. He turned to the two men and asked, "Is door muy malo?"

One of the men answered, "Maybe for five peso we can fix."

We suspected this was their way of earning money from the unsuspecting tourists. Although I was fuming as they unlocked the door, Jack just chuckled at the innovative way they discovered to make money. I didn't find it funny at all.

When I realized Laurie was writing the whole episode down for her teacher and her whole class to read, I was not amused. "Laurie, you don't have to write down everything."

She replied, "Momma, I promised!"

I appreciated her being honest, but after we arrived home, I discovered her journal had become a classic and her teacher refused to give it back to us. She showed it to a high school English teacher and then her husband, who was a teacher, took it to the Junior college where it was used as a perfect example of a composition. In a small community, this meant everywhere I went people smiled and asked about my experience. I found it rather humiliating.

After my experience with the port-a-pots, I was happy when we arrived in Guadalajara. We rented a luxurious motel suite, at reasonable rates. It consisted of three bedrooms and even better, three bathrooms besides the living quarters. At home, to go swimming, the children had to go to the river under strict supervision, but here Jackie and Laurie swam every day in the pool, while I became acquainted with the other parents. We became one large family.

After a couple of weeks, Jack and I decided we wanted to see Lake Chapala before leaving for home. We checked out of the motel, climbed in the car, and waved goodbye to our new friends. We were having a lovely drive when Jack noticed the car engine began to sputter as we started up a very slight incline. Jack's mechanical background told him to check the engine. He inspected the ignition, the fuel filter, and then the fuel pump. Jack discovered the diaphragm in the fuel pump was partially ruptured.

He decided to return to our friendly motel. We drove slowly, not sputtering as much as we did going up the incline. However, we were not sure we would reach the motel and Jack kept looking for a Toyota sign as we drove through town. We finally found one, but it was closed to business. At the motel, Jack discovered the Toyota Company had insulted the Mexican government, and they expelled Toyota from doing business. We also found out our best chance was to order the part we needed from Texas. We could have it sent down by bus which would take over a week.

We budgeted for six weeks in Mexico and felt we could afford that, but it seemed a terrible waste of money for us to stay in a motel for an extra week waiting for parts to arrive. We decided to pray about it. We put our faith and trust in God, and told Him our problem and how we really didn't want to stay any longer. We asked Him to provide us with a new diaphragm, thanked Him for listening to us and for answering our prayer.

The next morning Laurie and Jackie spread the word we planned on leaving with the damaged fuel pump.

We packed our suitcases, loaded the car up and made provisions to leave for home with a car that did not run well. The men said, "Do you realize when you leave here, you drive down into a canyon, and then you have a steep grade getting out? Your car will never make it. Going to Lake Chapala was a minor grade and you couldn't climb it! You came limping back. You're crazy if you leave here with your family. It's going to be much harder for you to come back tonight. Please don't do this."

The women implored me to try to talk sense to Jack and to accept the inevitable, relax and enjoy myself.

"Why are you doing this? You know your car can't make it. You'll be back again tonight."

Jack told them, "God wants us to have a nice vacation, but He also doesn't want us to waste our money having a longer vacation than we can afford. God will see us home."

We decided to pray in front of our new friends asking for God's care. We held hands and prayed, and when we said "Amen," Jackie climbed in the back seat. His eyes were large, but he never said a word. LaurieAnne also remained silent after our prayer and joined her brother.

Jack and I were quiet. Our faith never wavered knowing God could do this. The car ran fine on the down-hill grade, but as we started up the large mountain, it went slowly chug - chug - chug. It seemed as if God was testing us, but the higher we climbed, the faster the chug-chug-chug came until we hit the very steepest part of the mountain when it started purring like a kitten.

When we arrived in Texas I wanted Jack to stop and buy a new fuel pump, telling him,

"I only prayed to God to let us get to Texas where we could buy a new one."

Jack replied, "God never does anything halfway. He always finishes a job."

Our faith was rewarded and we had a wonderful trip home with no car trouble.

***

We continued to drive the Toyota for several years before we traded it in for a new car. Before Jack traded it, he told me, "I'm going to check that diaphragm again and see what it looks like." He came back in the house with a huge grin on his face, as he told me it looked like a brand new one, not one several years old. Just another one of God's many miracles!

ELSIE'S REQUEST

IT WAS THE EARLY 1960's and the cold war we were engaged in with Russia had us all living with the threat of the bomb. My children had drills at school where the teachers would sound an alarm and they would hide beneath their desks, to prepare them in case we received word an atom bomb was heading our way. The Russian Premier, Khrushchev, had threatened to "bury" America. It wasn't uncommon for new houses to come with the added feature of a bomb shelter in the backyard.

My mother-in-law, Elsie, and her sister, Kitty, took these worries to a level that would be called an obsession today. They wanted to be ready for an invasion by the Russians, which they were sure was imminent. They bought rain gear for each member of the family, along with boots, jackets, thermal underwear and heavy stockings. They also purchased gallons of honey, powdered milk for any babies, scissors, thread, needles, hand lotion, face cream, and other necessities they thought were needed. If they lived through the bomb blast and the invasion, they wanted to be ready!

These items were all stored in several steel barrels. They buried barrels of .22 rifles with ammunition on their land near Cave Junction, Oregon. Soon they also started burying paper money in glass jars, so no one would be able to find them with a metal detector. They spent a fortune buying massive amounts of grain and pouring it into gallon jars. After sealing the jars, they buried them in the ground.

They behaved like two teenagers, as they giggled, putting up all this grain. They had both been schoolteachers when they were younger. It surprised me watching them, as they were usually quite patrician in their actions. The two ladies were both beautiful, but in different ways. Elsie looked like an aristocrat, grace in every movement. Kitty was a year younger. She inspired feelings of protection in you, and you wanted to take care of her. When she smiled, you felt warmth fill your whole body.

The younger members of the family found all this exciting because Elsie and their Aunt Kitty made maps to show where everything was buried. We were given a copy of each map with strict orders they were to be hidden and only used in an emergency. The children thought they were going to have a great treasure hunt someday.

I tried to convince Elsie that, according to the Bible, when a man buries his treasure he would not be the one to enjoy it. Someone else would find it. I told her we must trust in God and let him take care of us in times of trouble.

Her reply was, "The Russians are coming, and we will have to flee to the hills to survive. We are going to have to be guerrillas and fight for our freedom. The guns are also for us to hunt deer to eat while we are in hiding. The Russians are going to invade the United States, and this will take care of us during the time it takes our government to win. The food is to live on, and I want my family to survive."

Elsie and Aunt Kitty were getting some subversive newspapers that kept them stirred up, and we couldn't reason with them. My husband adamantly refused to allow those newspapers into our home, and burned them when she mailed them to us.

I commented to Jack, "Your mom is just throwing her money

away. This is a terrible waste."

He replied, "It's my mother's money, and she has the right to use it anyway she wants to. If she wants to bury it or burn it, she can do it."

"But, Jack, your dad worked hard for some of this money before he died, and the rest you made for her in real estate."

"I know, Mona, but I am not going to tell my mother what to do with her money."

Since Elsie tithed her income and gave generously to the church, this shut me up. I couldn't argue the point any more, and faithfully took each map and put it in a safe place.

As the years went by without a Russian invasion, Kitty's husband, Gene, started secretly digging up the jars containing the money and spent it lavishly on "ladies of the night," and other foolish things.

However, the day came when Aunt Kitty needed money for an operation. Since they did not have health insurance, Uncle Gene had to confess he had dug the money up and spent it. There was only one jar of money left. They tried for days to find their buried treasure, looking at the map, but either the map was wrong, or Gene had reburied the money and forgotten where he'd put it.

One day, my mother-in-law, Elsie, telephoned me. "Mona, you're our last hope. Please come and find the jar of money for Kitty."

"What do you want me to do? Help them dig?"

Her answer was a surprise, and left me feeling stunned.

"Mona, God answers your prayers, and both Kitty and I feel you're the only hope she has of finding the money. Please drive to Cave Junction and ask God to help you find the money. Kitty is desperate and needs funds to pay for her operation."

How can you turn down a request like that? It also left me feeling apprehensive. I wondered if God would help me find the money, since I felt the women were not trusting in God when they buried it.

Elsie continued to plead with me. She and Aunt Kitty were extremely close, and Elsie felt protective of her younger sister. She sent money each month to make Kitty's life easier, since Kitty's husband, Gene, had never worked in all the years I knew them.

Aunt Kitty was an unusually sweet and loving person. Although she lived on a small teacher's pension, each month she bought a gift for my small children, LaurieAnne and Jackie. At Christmas they each received twelve little gifts from her, one for each month. She didn't see her great-niece and great-nephew often, but when she did, she always gave something to them. I felt I had to go, even if it meant digging with a shovel to try to find the money.

I first drove to Grants Pass, seventy miles from my home, to visit with Elsie, and reassure her I would do my best. She prayed with me, and then I drove another twenty miles to Cave Junction.

Arriving at Aunt Kitty's home, I could tell by the look on her face that she was stressed from the worry. She looked at me so hopefully. I did not want to disappoint her. I loved her very much, but I also realized this was going to be strictly up to God and His mercy.

I explained to Aunt Kitty and Uncle Gene, "We have to have a season of prayer in asking this favor of God, and you both have to believe God will show me where to find the money."

They looked so helpless as they agreed. We knelt in prayer, and in part of my prayer, I said, "Our Father, Aunt Kitty needs this money to pay for her surgery, and we are completely dependent on Your mercy in showing me where to look. Please guide me."

After we prayed, I felt confident I knew where to go, and I told them to follow me. Walking out the door, I turned left instead of right where they had been digging, walked about 200 feet, and pointed to a spot under a tree in the woods, and said, "The money is buried here." I stepped back, and waited for Uncle Gene to do his part.

Uncle Gene took his shovel and, after digging only a foot down, discovered the jar. We thanked God for restoring the money so needed for Kitty's medical needs.

I still feel humbled knowing God used me to find the hidden money for them.

GOD'S PROTECTIVE HAND

MY DAUGHTER, LAURIEANNE, and I decided to visit her grandmother. We started down Linden Ave, chatting, and when we arrived at Jefferson Blvd., we stopped at the red light. When it changed to green, I stepped on the gas, so I could turn left onto Jefferson Blvd. The car would not move. LaurieAnne gently said, "Mama, the light is green."

"I know, Honey."

"Well, why aren't you moving?"

"I can't."

"Why can't you? The drivers behind us are getting antsy."

"The car won't move."

"Why won't it?"

"I don't know. I have the gas pedal clear to the floor, and the car is in low gear, but for some odd reason, we aren't moving."

About this time a large eighteen-wheeler loaded with sugar beets came barreling through the red light. He would have wiped us out. We looked at each other, and started shaking. After he went through the red light, our car moved forward. We thanked God for sparing our lives.

We were so upset that we turned around and chased the truck until we were able to read its license plate. We called the highway patrol and told him what happened. He said, "I can't give him a ticket, but with the license and the name of the truck, I'm going down to talk to the owner."

We thanked him, turned around and started back to visit Laurie's grandmother.

After we entered the freeway, as we drove over the bridge, we could see a bad wreck on the other side. I kept my eyes on my side of the freeway. We soon realized the eighteen-wheeler beside us was looking at the wreck instead of the freeway, and was drifting into our lane. We were trapped by the traffic. There was a car driving just ahead of the engine of the truck, but not going any faster, and there was a car behind me, so I could not stop without risking being rear-ended. Laying on the horn didn't do any good.

LaurieAnne started praying out loud as we slowly drove closer to the side of the bridge over the river. I could hear LaurieAnne praying, "Oh, God, help us. Oh, God help us," over and over.

The driver was still looking at the wreck, when he glanced over and saw my car about to be crushed between him and the cement wall, or worse yet, forced over the wall into the Sacramento River. A shocked look came over his face, and he yanked his truck to the left.

Breathing a sigh of relief, we again thanked our Lord for His protection on our trip.

We drove the freeway talking about our near misses and how good God was to us. When we arrived at Watt Ave, I turned onto it. We drove a mile, when LaurieAnne started screaming, "Look out, Mom- look out!"

Since I was driving on a one-way street, with two lanes in my direction, I frantically looked around trying to see why she was warning me. There was a lawn division between us and the cars going in the opposite direction. 1 couldn't see anything wrong.

"Mom, pull over- pull over!"

I immediately pulled over to the right hand side of the street. Glancing across the street,

I could see the reason for her concern. A young boy who could barely see over the top of the steering wheel was driving too fast and clipped the side of a car, and lost control. He crossed the other two lanes of traffic, and started across the lawn in our direction.

He continued to drive up the little hill on my right, circled around the trees, came back down, barely missing us, crossed the divider and wiped out a car. After he hit this car, it spun his car around in a 180-degree turn in the middle of the street. He came back across the divider, crossed in front of us again, up the hill and back down, and over the divider and he hit another car. His car finally stopped. A young girl was standing by her wrecked car crying, and the young man in one of the other wrecked cars came and put his arms around her to comfort her. We heard the police siren, and knew someone called the police. After we realized everyone had climbed out of the four wrecked cars, we slowly drove on to visit my mother-in-law.

We felt as if Satan was trying to kill us, and again we thanked God for protecting us. We also asked God if we could please have a quiet trip home. We had enough excitement for one day.

I wonder why LaurieAnne always wants to drive when we go anywhere.

I know my guardian angel is the one who agitated me to the point I insisted we get in the slow lane.

TWO APPLES AND TWO SANDWICHES

I WAS EXCITED. My dreams had finally come true. My husband, Jack, and I, along with our two children, Laurie Anne, sixteen, Jack Jr., ten years old, and my niece, Margie Mansell, twenty-one years old, were in England. I had long dreamed of visiting the home of my ancestors, and here we were actually going to attend church at Newbold College in Berkshire.

Sabbath School was wonderful, as was the sermon, but no one went out of their way to make us feel welcome. After the service, however, I saw Dr. Seigfred Horn, a noted archeologist who had been a guest in our home in Oregon. When he saw us, he hurried over to greet us.

"Mona and Jack, how good to see you. Welcome to England."

After a few minutes of conversation, he said, "My wife and I would love to invite you home for dinner, but we've already accepted an invitation ourselves. If you're looking for a place to eat, visitors are always invited to dine at the cafeteria in the girls' dormitory."

We thanked Dr. Horn for the information. The friends we had been visiting in a nearby town had driven us to church, dropped us off, and returned home. We had assured them we would be able to eat after the service, since most of our churches have a potluck dinner for out-of-town guests. We discovered this wasn't the custom at Newbold, and we now had three hungry young people eager for something to eat.

We started off following Dr. Horn's directions to the girls' dormitory.

"I have a horrible feeling they're going to ask us for meal tickets," I told Jack.

"Oh, no," Jack said. "I don't think so. Dr. Horn said they always send all the guests over there to eat. It's probably where they have their potluck meal."

We walked in, picked up our trays and started down the food line.

A gentleman approached us and asked in a deep determined voice, "May I have your meal tickets?"

My worst fears were realized. I felt sick. In a small voice, I said, "No, Dr. Horn told us this is where they send visitors to eat after church."

"I don't care what Dr. Horn said, you have to have a meal ticket to eat here!"

"Can we eat, and then pay you after Sabbath?"

"No, you have to have a meal ticket. Please step out of line."

"A young woman spoke up and said, "Please let them eat. They're visitors and can use my meal ticket."

"No, they can't. They have to have their own meal ticket," the guardian of the food line insisted.

The cashier then spoke up. "Please let them eat. I'll pay for their meals after sundown."

"NO! I said they have to have their own meal ticket!" By now this overly zealous individual was angry with all of us, and my feelings were hurt. We always took strangers into our home and fed them. I was so disappointed, I just wanted to leave.

I was concerned. In order to reach church on time, none of us had eaten any breakfast.

We had assured our friends who brought us, we would return home by train. However, the train we needed didn't leave until 6:30 p.m. and it would be 8:30 p.m. before we reached our friends' home. The children were all hungry and clamoring for something to eat. We needed to find food, but where?

As we were leaving the cafeteria, the young woman who wanted to let us use her meal ticket approached us, carrying a small brown paper bag. She said, "I just wasn't hungry after you were told you couldn't eat in the cafeteria, so I got a sack lunch. If you are willing to come up to my room, I'd love to share my lunch with you."

I knew this generous young woman couldn't possibly have enough food to feed all of us, but she insisted.

"Please come to my room. I live in Romania, behind the Iron Curtain. I miss my parents and have not had any company since I came to school. Now I can't go home because of the political situation. I miss my mother, and you look like my mother. Please come and share my lunch with me."

I looked into her eyes and could not refuse her. I looked at my husband and the three children. They either shrugged their shoulders or said, "Why not?"

So, we went to the girls' dorm. It didn't look like our modern nice dorms in Oregon. It had been converted from an old mansion. It needed repairs, but had a homey atmosphere. The rooms for the students were quite small and cramped, however. There was one small cot, a desk, and one chair. We sat on the floor. Our hostess asked Jack to say the blessing on the food.

As we started to eat, there was a knock on the door and in came the cashier. She said she felt so terrible about our being turned away and not allowed to eat, she had decided to get a sack lunch and join us for lunch. Both girls were from Romania. They informed us they didn't have much to eat at home, but they always shared what they had with guests.

The girls urged, "Will you play Mama and divide the food for us?"

There were now seven of us. I spread out the food. We had two apples and two peanut butter sandwiches. I divided the two apples into seven pieces and the two sandwiches into seven pieces. Each person received a very small piece of each.

We ate our food slowly, savoring each bite. We talked about Jesus and how much He loves us. We talked about the prayers He has answered for us. These girls were no longer able to return home, so we prayed for their families.

This turned out to be one of the most wonderful, memorable Sabbaths of my life. The Lord certainly blessed our food, because at the end of the meal, none of us were hungry. Not even my young son, Jackie, who always seemed to have a bottomless pit for a stomach.

We had been blessed to meet two young girls who were willing to share what little they had with us, and it was Jesus who did the rest. We were all completely satisfied and felt we had received a special blessing from God. I could finally better understand how Jesus had divided the fish and bread and fed over 7,000 with so little.

When I looked at my tall husband who likes his food, and my growing son, who seemed to be hungry all the time, and realized that all of us were left with a full and satisfied tummy, I could only thank God for his goodness and mercy.

I still marvel at how God fed seven of us on the Sabbath day with just two peanut butter sandwiches and two apples.

UPSTAGED

My pastor, Frank Hightower, and my head elder, Steve Wood, scheduled me to perform the 11:00 o'clock sermon. They requested I tell one of my miracle stories about my guardian angel. This gave me a whole month to prepare, but also time to get nervous as the day approached.

Last week, my friend Janna, who is the Religious Liberty Leader, realizing the offering was for Religious Liberty, announced, "I'm going to preach next week."

I told her, "I'm scheduled for the 11-clock time."

She asked, "How much of the sermon time are you going to give me to talk about religious liberty?"

"You better talk to Steve, and perhaps he will schedule me for next month."

Steve said, "You can take the time between Sabbath School and Church, but Mona is scheduled for the sermon."

She sent me an e-mail again, asking, "How much time can I have during the sermon time?"

I e-mailed her to talk to Steve. Steve telephoned me and said, "She asked me about sermon time again, and I told her she could talk but not during the sermon time. I finally gave her twenty minutes."

After he received another e-mail, again requesting how much time during the sermon she could have, he raised it to twenty-five minutes. He said, "I had to give her twenty-five minutes, Mona. I'm sorry. However, I told her it had to be between Sabbath School and church time, and not from the pulpit."

When the big day arrived, the preliminaries dragged on and on. My nerves began to act up.

I sat on the front row with the others who would be walking out on the platform. After talking about Religious Liberty from the floor, Janna decided to climb up behind the pulpit and preach a sermon. She started with the Tree of Knowledge in the Garden of Eden, and talked about the Good Samaritan, and ended up in Revelation. She covered the whole Bible. She read many Bible texts that had nothing to do with Religious Liberty. I started looking at my watch wondering if I should even try to talk. Elder Steve came and whispered in my ear, "I'm so sorry. You take the full time allotted for the sermon."

My nervous system caused my hands to shake. I wanted to get my miracle story behind me.

When Janna finished, the others who were to give the prayer and scripture reading and I walked back to the study room and briefly prayed. When we walked out on the platform, I glanced at the clock and thought, *I think I better shorten my story.*

When the children's story started, my little two-year-old, great-great-granddaughter, Catalina, came up front for the reading. She decided she wanted her Nana. Amused chuckles broke out in the audience as she climbed up the stairs to my lap, and I held her all through the children's story. She sat quietly as she stared out at the vast audience. I couldn't help wondering if this tiny tyke would remember this moment.

The children's story is supposed to take from three to five minutes, but the story lasted closer to eight minutes. When I started to breathe a sigh of relief, this dear sister next decided to read to the children for several minutes from a paper she held in her hands. My nerves were now stretched to the max, and beginning to affect my stomach. Glancing at the clock, I saw it was now five minutes to twelve, and people like to get out of church around noon. I wondered if I should just pray and dismiss church, but when I looked out over the audience, I saw too many family members who came to hear "Grandma" for the first time.

After the children's story, my three-year-old granddaughter, Chase, patiently stood there waiting for a basket to take up the children's offering. The small baskets are kept in a large laundry basket, with handles on each side. When Chase realized there were no baskets left for her, she picked up the laundry basket which was larger than herself. She staggered a little as she carried it down the aisle for the offering. The church members started laughing, and the men started reaching back into their wallets.

She collected more money with that oversized basket than the little ones before her. This money is used exclusively to send children to places like summer camp, the zoo, or Marine World.

My daughter, LaurieAnne, sang *My Guardian Angel Walks With Me*, and the song started to help me relax.

At seven minutes after twelve, when the church should be out, I stood up to talk. I talked for twenty minutes, so we finished church at 12.30. My oldest son wore a big smile on his face as he listened for the first time to his mother tell one of her miracle stories in church.

Tonight I am wondering which the congregation will remember— my sermon, or two-year-old Catalina insisting on sitting on my lap up on the platform, or three-year-old Chase taking up the offering in a laundry basket.

I think they upstaged me.

30

"O LORD my God, I cried unto thee, and thou hast healed me."
Psalm 30:2

THE KIND PHYSICIAN

I HAD BEEN FEELING ILL for some time, but as a member of Kaiser, this meant getting up before 6 A.M. in order to get an appointment, hopefully with my own, wonderful, Dr. Link. I had not been able to see him in several of my recent appointments, and each time had to take a different doctor.

When I made this appointment, once again, I was told Dr. Link was not available, but I could get in to see Dr. Klingbeil.

When Dr. Klingbeil entered the room, a feeling of peace and well being came in with him. He gave me a sweet smile, and his eyes were soft and compassionate. I really don't quite know how to describe him, except I felt better just being in his presence.

He held my charts in his hands, as he asked me why I wanted to see a doctor, and after checking my chart, but before examining me, he looked up and gave me a smile. When I told him my symptoms, he told me that my doctor had prescribed the wrong medication, and he believed if I was on a different prescription, I would be better. He wrote one out for me, and went on to tell me I would improve in twenty-four hours. He had such a charming presence I was beginning to feel better already, I became so confident when I left, after filling the prescription, I told Jack, "If I hadn't been about fifteen years with Dr. Link and was happy with him, I would ask for Dr. Klingbeil to be my primary care doctor."

Jack asked me what was so special about Dr. Klingbeil, and I told him, "I think the way he made me feel. It was as if I was special to him. Strange, as I had never seen him before, but he wore a certain glow to him and such a sweet and loving smile, I really knew he cared for me."

About 3 months later, I needed to see a doctor again, and when I telephoned once again I was told Dr. Link was not available today. She mentioned several other doctors, and I said, "That's okay—I'd like to see Dr. Klingbeil again."

She replied, "We don't have a Dr. Klingbeil on our staff."

I was indignant, and told her, "Why I saw him three months ago, and he is wonderful."

She answered, "I can see on your chart a Dr. Klingbeil treated you, but he is not listed."

Again, I came back, "He not only saw me, but he gave me a prescription and the pharmacy filled it. I felt better almost immediately after I took it." I gave her the prescription number.

The advice nurse said, "Let me call the pharmacy." When she got back to me, she quietly said, "They said they filled that prescription, alright, but they have no other record of him. This is strange. Let me call the emergency room and see if he ever moonlighted for them."

I waited, and soon she came back on the line and quietly said, "They have never heard of him. I want to get to the bottom of this. I am going to call the administration."

When she came back to me, she quietly said in an awed voice, "They have never heard of him. I have never known of this happening before. This is a little unnerving. I wonder who the doctor was..."

I couldn't help but feel, once more, my guardian angel had stepped in to make sure I got the right medicine.

PANIC

MY DAUGHTER, LAURIE, and I were on our way to Fort Bragg to visit my sister, Lillian. Laurie was driving a steady seventy miles-per-hour and doing a fine job. I always felt safe with her at the wheel and never felt the need to do any backseat driving.

The shadows reflecting on the mountains from the setting sun were beautiful. While enjoying the scenery, I started to get a very uncomfortable feeling, a vague sense of unease. Soon the sensation grew stronger, and I couldn't resist this intuition of danger any longer.

"Laurie, I think you should move over in the slow lane."

Laurie replied, "I will as soon as there is an opening."

A mounting sense of foreboding filled me. I started insisting she move now! She replied, "Mom, I can't until a car gives us room. I'm signaling."

This feeling became so overpowering I couldn't keep quiet, and I started nagging her, "Laurie, we have to move over now."

The urgency to move gripped me. The feeling began to consume me, and I could not relax.

Laurie was trying, but there was no opening, even with her signaling, and I gave her no peace. I became overwhelmed with fear, and insisted she get in the slow lane.

"Now, Laurie- move now!" I commanded her. Unreasoning panic filled me, and this became an urgent, terrifying feeling. I kept glancing in the rear view mirror, watching the headlights of the cars behind us. The feeling of danger was so strong, and I could not see any way Laurie would be able to manage to get in the next lane. I became terrified.

"Force your way in- Laurie, you have to move over now! MOVE IT! MOVE IT! NOW!" I started shouting at her.

Laurie, without arguing with me, managed to force our car into the slow lane. However, this did not satisfy me. I still felt antsy, with this strange, compelling feeling of danger that stayed with me. I turned around to look out the back window, and I started watching the headlights of the cars in the fast lane, behind us. I started sputtering to Laurie, "Why doesn't that truck pass us? He HAS to pass us. Please hurry and pass us. Please pass us."

Laurie quietly told me, "Mom, I don't know why he doesn't pass us, but he is slowly creeping up on us."

My consuming compulsion for this truck to be in front of us, was so strong, I knew we were in immediate danger.

"Slow down, Laurie—slow down so that truck is forced to get in front of us."

"Mom, I'm trying to slow, but with this heavy traffic, I have to slowly ease up on the gas."

Now Laurie not only was driving in heavy traffic at seventy-miles-per-hour, but she had a frantic mother in the front seat telling her how to drive. Nervously, I kept saying, more to myself than to Laurie, "That truck has to pass us. Please hurry and pass us."

Laurie felt her mother had become instantly senile, and in a consoling voice, tried to comfort me. "He is beginning to pass us now, Mom."

As I watched the truck drive ahead of us, I leaned back and

started to relax. When the engine of his truck was three feet in front of our car, a huge, white animal leaped over the divider between the north and south highway. The truck hit it, and its body came sailing across into our lane. It looked like a horse or an elk. My mind was stunned at the size of it and its white color, and I was not sure what I was seeing.

Laurie was now trying to maneuver around this animal, as it spun in circles on its back, down the highway in front of us. This was the craziest thing I have ever seen in my life. Laurie did an expert job of driving and missing the dead animal. It continued to lay down on its back, with its legs straight up in the air, and whirled around in circles, traveling down the highway.

When we were out of danger, reality hit us. Laurie repeatedly said, "Mom, we would have been killed in this little Honda if we had hit that huge beast. I'm so glad you taught me, when I was young, to instantly obey your command."

Laurie repeated this several times. We thanked God for saving our lives. We also thanked God for our guardian angel, who gave me this strong sense of urgency to move into the other lane, and to have the truck act as a buffer between this strange creature and us.

***

When Laurie and I arrived in Willits, I telephoned my nephew, Wayne Miller, in Ukiah, Ca., and told him about this strange creature and what happened. He told me that a wealthy rancher imported huge, white deer from Europe and there were now three herds of them. He immediately told me where I almost hit the deer, as they had terrible accidents take place there. The highway had been built as a deer crossing on a mountain.

32

OPERATION GALLANT EAGLE

MY SON, LARRY, a chaplain and a paratrooper in the 82nd Airborne, wanted us to see what he called a magnificent panorama. Excitedly, my other two sons drove me to Fort Irwin, where we would be able to see all the action.

When we arrived at the deployment area, Harold and Jack deserted me, and headed off to watch the panorama in their chosen spots. An officer who knew me approached and indicated I should climb this small hill. Pointing to a colonel, he said, "Go over there by that officer, and you'll be able to see Larry jump." He went on to tell me after today, he would be one of Larry's enemies in the mock war. After he made sure I was heading where I could see Larry fly in, he trotted off in a totally different direction. Climbing the hill, I went over and stood near the colonel. News photographers surrounded us, all focused toward the eastern horizon. I was the only civilian standing with the military.

The darkness was slowly fading as dawn approached. *How much longer?* I wondered, and as if in reply to my thoughts, the officer standing next to me said, "They will appear at 6:07. Look right there, Ma'am," he pointed to the eastern sky. "They will appear over the mountains."

"Will we see different colors?" I asked. Larry told me he would be in the silver airplanes.

I was curious how I would know Larry's group of planes, as they were flying in from all over the United States.

"Yes, Ma'am," he patiently replied. "The rising sun reflecting on the airplanes as they fly in from different parts of the United States will give us three different colors. The airplanes to the left will appear gold. The airplanes to the right will look like lead, but our boys, Ma'am, they'll be in the Silver Birds." Someway, he seemed to know if I was standing by him, we were waiting for the same airplanes. I knew then I had found the right officer.

Wishing I had brought a warmer coat, I shivered. Since the war operations were taking place in the desert, I naturally thought the desert would be Warm. The air felt as if it was blowing over an iceberg, as it hit us in icy gales. As we watched, the officer, the camera crew, and myself, we all shivered in the cold desert air. I could no longer keep my teeth from chattering, and from time to time, I felt my body shudder from the cold.

In the far distance, a fire appeared to be lit and red smoke wafted in swirls of air on the desert floor. My kind officer explained to me, "As long as the smoke is red, they won't jump, it's too windy, and too dangerous. Looks like part of today's big practice will be cancelled. Your son won't jump."

He spoke in short, brusque sentences.

"What will happen to him, if he doesn't jump?" I found myself pleading, "They won't send him back to North Carolina, will they? I will get to see him, won't I?"

A disappointed feeling swept through me, and I needed reassuring. It had been a long two years since I had set my eyes on my beloved son.

"Oh, they will fly over the field, Ma'am."

Pointing, he said, "He'll land over there. Just go to the chapel, where he said he would meet you. But stay and watch the others jump. The Gold and Lead will jump, because their landing field is less windy, but not the Silver. Your son would want you to see this demonstration, but he won't jump. They won't let him jump. It's much too windy, Ma'am. Much too dangerous."

I wondered how he knew Larry had told me to meet him at the chapel. I had not mentioned to him Larry was a chaplain. Had I possibly met him when I went to visit Larry? Whenever I visited my son, he always proudly introduced me to his superior officers, but I didn't remember seeing this man. I also didn't understand why the landing fields for the Gold and the Lead would be less windy, but I did not press for an answer.

As time passed, my officer seemed to get a little edgy.

"What color is the smoke now, Ma'am?"

"It is red, sir," I replied.

I wondered why he asked me. Couldn't he see for himself? Maybe he was color blind, or maybe he had forgotten to bring his glasses. He was so kind to me, answering any questions I asked in the predawn light. I felt a rapport with him, but I noticed a tension building in his body. I strained my eyes, looking for the first glimpse of the Silver Birds in the sky.

'What color is the smoke, ma'am? I can hear the planes coming," he asked, beginning to sound anxious. He acted as if he was not sure whether our boys would jump or not.

"It is red, sir," I responded.

He appeared to heave a sigh of relief. The planes appeared on the horizon, skimming the mountaintops. Gold planes to the left, Lead planes to the right, and the Silver planes coming toward us. My heart thrilled at the sight. My heart started pounding with the excitement of knowing I soon would be able to see my precious son today. It had been a long time, since I had seen him, and I was so excited over the prospect of once more holding my son in my arms.

Impatiently, the officer turned to me, and once more asked, "What color is the smoke now, Ma'am?"

I looked and answered, "It is white, sir."

He stiffened, and I could feel him tense up. I saw parachutes begin to unfold in the windy sky above us.

"Sir, you told me they wouldn't jump." I looked at him accusingly. "You said it would be too dangerous."

"Ma'am, those are just supplies, falling with their parachutes. You notice the parachutes open immediately. We need the jeeps and the other supplies, so they fall first. They won't let the boys jump. It is much too dangerous."

I returned to enjoy watching the parachutes as they opened and began to fall. They looked like white mushrooms falling from the sky, with the stems pointing downwards. They were landing all over the desert. I marveled at the army's ingenuity in their organization of providing food, equipment and even jeeps, for the men to drive. It was thrilling to watch this army maneuver unfold. Suddenly his voice sounded strained, he turned to me and urgently asked, "What color is the smoke, Ma'am?"

I turned and looked across at the distant smoke on the desert floor, and felt my heart plummet.

Quietly I answered, "It is green, sir."

"Oh, God," he desperately said, and I knew it was a prayer from my kind officer. I started praying for my son. My son was jumping, and I knew it was too dangerous. I watched as the parachutes came tumbling out.

Falling ... falling ... falling.

They were beautiful as they opened. A sense of awe came over me, as I watched the soldiers descend. There were thousands of billowing parachutes all over the sky. Larry had told me he would be the first to jump out of his plane. I anxiously prayed until all the boys' parachutes opened from this first Silver plane. A sense of relief came over me. I snapped pictures for Larry's photo album. Until, that is, the first parachute did not open from the second plane. The soldier seemed to hurtle through the air, and my first thoughts were, *Is it Larry? Oh, God, please don't let it be Larry.*

I prayed desperately for his chute to open. It didn't, then I prayed his reserve would open, and when I grasped the knowledge it would not open either, I knew he had only seconds to live. Shock filled me. Fear tormented me. Was I watching my own son fall to his death? What desperation and terror he must have been feeling, as he plummeted to the ground. Agony filled my soul.

When I had asked Larry why he would be the first to jump out of whatever plane he was on, he told me it seemed to give the soldiers confidence to jump, if the chaplain went first. I tried to reassure myself, it was not my son. Larry had said he MIGHT be the first to jump out of his plane. But what if he wasn't? Doubt filled me. I did not want this first soldier to jump out of his plane to be my son. I felt selfish praying it would not be my son, and reproached myself. Some mother would grieve this night. Would it be me?

Was this boy ready to meet God? I prayed for his soul, as I watched him plunge toward the ground, as his unopened chute streamed in a straight, flat line above him.

The impact when he hit the ground seemed to send shock waves through my body. I continued to pray for him, after he hit the ground. My insides were tied in knots and I still felt as if I could feel his body slamming into the hard ground. I wanted to vomit. I wondered could anyone live through this kind of impact.

I prayed for his family, and for all the men jumping. I prayed for my son without ceasing.

I prayed and prayed. All the glory and excitement were gone. My insides were in torment. Only fears remained. It hurt inside too much to even cry. I was in shock, watching a man die before my eyes, and knowing it might be my own son.

I watched for the ambulance. I hoped this soldier was still alive, and maybe they might save his life. I still clung to this impossible wish. It seemed to take an eternity for the ambulance to start and drive over toward him.

What if he is still alive and suffering? I questioned in my mind.

I tried to hurry the ambulance with my mind and mentally tried to push it faster. It seemed to be crawling. Everything seemed to have gone into slow motion. I felt I could have run to this man faster than the ambulance was driving. His parachute did not blow across the desert like the other men, despite the high wind. He just lay there, on the ground, with the parachute still unopened, yet vertically knifing straight into the sky above him.

I wondered why the other soldiers were being dragged across the desert with their parachute open, but the dead soldier's parachute just hung over him like a sword. I tried to avoid looking at him, but everywhere my eyes moved, I seemed to see this fallen soldier with the anchored parachute, billowing tall as a fir tree on the desert floor. I looked left and right, but my eyes could still see this fallen hero.

Up into the sky was a vast panorama filled with men still falling to the earth, most floating safely, but as I watched in horror, another chute did not open, and I felt bile rise up in my throat. It was worse than watching a horror movie, because this was real life, and I could not just walk away. Some soldiers behind me in uniform joked about death. They joked about the chutes not opening, about the others meeting death. "Another one bites the dust."

I struggled to keep from screaming at them. "One of those dead boys may be my son." As they continued their callous comments, my back stiffened, as I stood by the colonel. He glanced at me. I looked at him. I didn't say a word. I didn't want my son to be disgraced by his mother losing control, possibly in front of his own colonel, but he must have seen the anguish in my eyes as I fought to control my emotions. I know his face reflected the horror he was feeling.

The boys chattered on about death, about the paratrooper biting the dust, about the dead boys. "There's three dead," they said, as if they are watching a video game. The officer ignored them. I decided if he could, so could I.

I gathered strength from the colonel's conduct. He didn't pull rank, and tell them to be quiet, it was as if both of us felt forced to pretend we did not hear these insensitive, callow privates. All I knew was their words were like knives, cutting away at my self-control.

I must not embarrass my son. I repeated this over and over to myself.

I continued praying over and over, for my son, and for all the boys jumping. Soon the chattering, immature soldiers left. I hoped they had been trying to hide their feelings. They probably had never seen death before. Maybe they thought the excitement was over, but I knew the worst was taking place now, right in front of my eyes, still going on.

The gusting winds had increased, and I saw parachutes being dragged through the desert. The men dragged across the ground, encountered rocks and cacti, and the men still jumping out of the airplanes were landing on the jeeps and other equipment dropped earlier. I knew more men were being injured, and were dying. I remembered what my son had told me, "Mom, wind is a paratrooper's worst enemy."

I knew the injuries were multiplying. My heart cried for the soldiers being dragged through the cactus. It wept for the young dead—soldiers too young to die. Now, of the ones who lived, many would be seriously hurt, some maimed for life.

I pleaded with God, "Please spare these boys, Lord. No more deaths, God. Please no more deaths. I can't bear to see any more killed. They are so young. God, please stop this wind!"

I could not leave; it was as if I was cemented to the spot. I was watching the carnage taking place, and I was being torn inside. My heart felt as if it was being ripped apart, watching more young men landing hard on equipment, dying, and being dragged by the wind.

Helicopters were beginning to land. They were loading up the injured and flying off. They, too, seemed to be in slow motion. Ambulances were driving out to the desert. I could see puffs of dust trailing behind, so I knew it was only in my mind they were slowly traveling. I wanted them to get to the injured immediately.

I watched the parachutes still dragging our boys through cactus. It was like watching a horror movie you had to stay and finish, but this was no horror movie. It was too real, and more terrifying. My imagination played havoc with my thoughts. I imagined my son being hurt and laying out in the desert. Intense pain gripped me. I held my stomach with my fist, trying to control the pain within my heart.

Everyone had left except the camera crew and my officer and me. He looked at me with sympathy in his eyes, and quietly suggested,

"Ma'am, I think we should leave now."

I did not want to leave as long as I could see the men still being dragged across the desert by parachutes, which refused to be released. Men were dying before my eyes.

All I could see were bodies still being dragged through the desert, and in my heart, I knew my son is still out there. I tried to hide my tears.

The kind colonel turned, and took my arm, leading me away from the nightmare scene of desolation and death. The camera crew had packed up and left. Only the colonel and I were now left standing on the lonely hilltop. I allowed the colonel to lead me, and when he let go of my arm, the wind seemed to blow me down the hill. I met my two sons, Harold and Jack, at our car. Too horrified by our fears to talk to each other, it was a silent drive to the chapel. We were afraid to give voice to our terror.

We were supposed to have met Larry here, at the chapel, about forty-five minutes after he jumped. I waited on the hill for what seemed hours, watching the disaster take place, and he was not at the chapel.

Now my worries hit me harder. The minutes ticked by, the hours slowly passed. We watched the medi-vacs still flying overhead, filled with injured and dying, and flying them to hospitals in the Los Angeles area. There was a huge tent set up on the grounds for the seriously injured, and it was filled with hundreds of more men, waiting for medical attention.

The ambulances went screaming past us, bringing more injured in from the desert, and we watched them speeding back to the desert. Still, we waited. Praying. Thinking. Wondering. Were we waiting for a man who would never arrive?

We waited and watched and silently prayed. I couldn't help thinking, *Is my son dead or alive?* The thought repeated itself over and over in my mind.

A long five hours slowly ticked by, as we paced around the grounds of the chapel. We passed each other, and did not look into each other's eyes, afraid of what we would see. My two sons and I didn't even speak to each other. We glanced at each other from time to time, each of us afraid of our own thoughts. There was no other person at the chapel. The three of us were alone in our misery. We refused to even think about leaving, without knowing what had happened to Larry. We glanced at our watches, stopped and drank from the water fountain, and continued our pacing back and forth.

Finally a jeep drove up, and a camouflaged soldier wearily climbed out. The jeep drove away. The exhausted soldier walked slowly toward us with a defeated air, shoulders drooping, as if he could barely put one foot in front of the other. He looked as if he was dreading giving the news he had come to deliver. My heart plummeted against the brief hope it held, when I saw the jeep drive into our area.

Yet there was something about this walk, and again my heart started beating faster. Could it be my Larry?

I joyously commenced to run to meet him. Then I stopped. The camouflage was too great. My heart cried, because I didn't know if it was my son. Who was this camouflaged soldier? Was he a soldier bearing bad news? Can he be my son? I had seen Larry in fatigues before, when he would come in from the field, but there was something about this soldier I had never seen in my son. I had seen him tired, but never with this defeated walk. Shoulders drooping, he slowly put one foot in front of the other.

Harold and Jack didn't run to meet him either, so doubt filled me, and I felt my heart plunging against the hope it briefly held. I was afraid he was coming to tell me my son was dead. Suddenly he opened his arms wide, so I ran, with rejoicing in my heart. Larry enveloped me in his arms, and oh, it felt so good. I didn't know if he was holding me, or if I was holding him, but Larry was alive. I wanted to shout and cheer with my happiness in knowing,

MY SON IS ALIVE!

My heart was singing with happiness, until I drew back, and looked him over. There was fresh blood streaming down the side of his face. A patch of hair was missing from Larry's head. His hand looked broken.

I exclaimed, "Oh, my darling you're hurt!"

He looked at me with eyes that had seen death, and lived.

"No, Mom, I'm not hurt. I'm the only one not hurt in the Silver Drop Zone, I think."

I searched my son's face. He stood before me in shock, almost bereft of words. His eyes reflected the heart wrenching horror he had been through. He laid his head on my shoulder and shuddered, as his voice broke in anguish, "Oh, Mom, They're dead. My friends are all dead. I held my Sarge in my arms as he died. He landed on a truck, and broke his back. Oh, Mom, My Sarge is dead."

He gave another gulp, and then brokenly said, "A young lieutenant and I were being dragged across the desert together, and talking, and then he went silent, and when I got to him, his neck was broken. Oh, Mom - it was horrible."

I had forgotten, as a chaplain, he would stay with the wounded. I wanted to comfort him, but I couldn't. What could I say to this man, who had just seen so much more of death in one day than I ever had in my life? All I could do was grieve for him in the loss of his friends, and tell him I was sorry. I also said a quiet prayer of thanks, selfishly rejoiced in my heart: this man, my son, is alive. This soldier. This gentleman. This son of mine, HE IS ALIVE!

***

Larry drove us to the big tent, where we waited again while he went back to talk to his commanding officer, for further orders. He told us there were hundreds of injured soldiers lying in this huge triage tent, with broken arms, broken legs, and other injuries they considered minor. The army was flying these soldiers back to North Carolina immediately. This was deliberate, so the number of causalities would not be known by the news media. The most serious were being sent to the local hospitals. He was assigned to drive to Loma Linda Hospital where the most critical head injuries were sent. I tagged along with him down the hospital halls, as he went into each room to pray and comfort the injured. He went into the operating room with one soldier, and later he came out with a grim look, and told me "Mom, I lost another one of my men." It was hard seeing my son grieve over the loss of each of his men. To this day, I cannot get the picture out of my mind of the soldiers dying. I still have nightmares.

AUSTIN AND GOD

MY DAUGHTER, LAURIEANNE, married a young man, Michael, with two sons. Three-year-old Cody had blond hair with curly locks and blue eyes. He was, and still is, very hyperactive. He doesn't know what being still means. Austin was four, with light brown, wavy hair, and green eyes. Austin is a little more serious and very dependable. Both of the boys looked like little cherubs.

Laurie and Michael had the boys during the week and one weekend a month. During the weekends Michael has his boys, and he likes to spend quality time with them, like taking them camping. This means LaurieAnne seldom has any time to take them to church. For many years, she read Bible stories when she tucked them into bed at night while their father read them fantasy stories when it was his turn. This worried my daughter because she felt the boys didn't have enough religious training.

LaurieAnne became concerned because as they grew older her stepson, Austin, denied God existed.

"Mom, it's hard to convince a ten-year-old there is a God. Would you try to talk to him and tell him about how much Jesus loves him?"

"Of course, LaurieAnne, I'll be glad to."

Talking didn't do any good. No matter how I explained and told Austin of Jesus' love, he would give me a little smirk, and say, "You haven't proved anything yet—how can I believe in something that doesn't exist? You have to prove to me there's a God. I put him in the same category as Santa Claus. I used to believe in Santa Claus and look what happened. He doesn't exist. So why should I believe in God?"

This left me baffled, and all I could do was pray, "God, show me how to reach this boy, so he will learn to love you."

I tried, but with no more success than LaurieAnne.

One day Laurie and the boys came to see me and she was distraught. "Mom, I lost my wallet. Please pray I'll get it back. I know where I left it. I took the boys out for a hamburger after school, and I paid for the sandwiches, and left the wallet lying on the counter. I just drew a hundred out of the bank to pay a bill I owe, and Mom, you know I can't afford to lose that much money."

"Let's pray, Laurie. God can restore your wallet."

This comforted Laurie, and they left to drive back across town to the restaurant. When they left, Laurie was smiling, as she felt confident God would restore her wallet. However, in about an hour they returned, Laurie in tears. The restaurant manager told her, "We're too busy to notice who picked up your wallet. We don't have time to see who leaves wallets here."

The thought crossed my mind; maybe this is the way to prove to Austin there is a God.

I asked Austin, "If God answers my prayer and the wallet is found, will you believe in God?"

He gave me a cocky smile, "Sure."

In my prayer, I asked God to restore Laurie's wallet to her in such a way it would convince Austin that God existed. I thanked Him for answering my prayer.

When we were through praying and stood up, Austin gave me a pitying look. His facial expression was, *I feel sorry for you, Nana, you really believe this, and God doesn't exist. Poor Nana.*

I smiled and kissed him on the cheek and commented, "Austin, you're going to see God perform a miracle."

In a worried tone of voice, Laurie asked, "Mom, aren't you putting God in a difficult position?"

"No. God tells us to prove him, and I was just giving God the opportunity to prove to Austin that He existed."

Austin flashed his feeling-sorry-for-you look at me.

Later that day, Austin came in with a radiant smile on his face. "Nana, I found the wallet!"

"Where was it, Austin?"

"It was in my backpack in the trunk of the car. I found it when I started to do my homework. And I know Laurie left it in the restaurant. So how did it get in the trunk of the car, and in my backpack that I hadn't opened since I left school?"

"Do you think maybe God put it there?"

He gave me a serious look, "Yes, Nana, but why in my backpack? Why not in Cody's?"

"Does Cody believe in God?"

"Yes, Nana."

"Who said they didn't believe in God?"

"I did, Nana."

"Don't you suppose God put it in your backpack, so you would believe in Him? Do you believe in God now, Austin?"

He replied with a firm, "Yes, Nana, I do."

It wasn't only LaurieAnne and her sons who felt like rejoicing. My husband commented, "It's good to know God is still performing miracles in this family."

***

Austin, sixteen at the time of this writing and over six feet tall, plays his guitar in church for me whenever I request him to play for special music. He is very handsome, and still has that charming smile that bewitched me when he was four years old. I love this step-grandson very much.

CODY AND GOD

MY DAUGHTER'S STEPSON, CODY, is a typical teenager. He can out-argue anyone, and should study to be a lawyer. He completely frustrates his father, until Michael is furious. He pushes my daughter, LaurieAnne, until she is in tears, yet he is sweet, loving, and considerate of me.

Cody just turned eighteen, and graduated from high school. His mother had joint custody of him until he was sixteen. Michael went to court twice trying to obtain full custody, as Cody's mother introduced all three of her sons to marijuana. She finally signed over custody papers to Cody's father, since she has a little girl now, and no time for him. He came to live full-time with LaurieAnne, and her husband, when he was sixteen. Each time I have managed to talk Cody into going to church, he has arrived looking different. One time his hair was colored black, another time it was green, and once it was blue.

When he came to church one Sabbath, I was up on the platform. He arrived late, surprising me. I was so happy to see him; I walked down from the pulpit and hugged him. Of course the service came to a stop and there were chuckles throughout the room. This time his hair was arranged into tight little braids called dreadlocks.

After church, a beautiful, African-American lady, went up to Cody and laughingly asked, "Are you deliberately trying to embarrass your grandmother? I know what those braids mean."

She told me he became embarrassed and hung his head. She went on to tell him, "Obviously, no matter what you do, it is not going to affect her love for you. You might as well give up and cut your long hair and let it grow naturally."

The next time I saw Cody, his hair was short, blond and wavy.

I knew Cody would resent me if I called him too often to go to church, so I only asked about once a month. One week, I telephoned and asked, "Cody, will you go to church with me this Sabbath?"

"I can't, Nana. I have a job now, and I work weekends."

"Cody, I think I'll pray and ask God to rearrange your hours at the restaurant, so you can come to church."

"If He does, I'll come." He felt safe promising this. Then he added, "But you know, I don't believe in God."

"I know better, Cody. I know you've been reading the Bible I gave you, because when you come, you answer more of the questions asked than the members do. You're intelligent enough if you wanted to, you could teach a Bible class."

He chuckled. "That'll be the day, Nana!"

Two days later, LaurieAnne called and said, "Mom, Cody broke his foot and can't work for six weeks. I think he'd like you to call him and give him a little Grandma love and sympathy."

After commiserating with my boy on the phone, I cheerfully told him, "Since you can't work now, you can come to church with me."

There was silence on the line and then, in a very serious tone of voice, he asked me, "Did you ask God to break my foot so I'd come to church?"

This struck my funny bone, coming from a boy who professed not to believe in God. Giggling, I answered, "I never asked God to break your foot! That's His own sense of humor! All I asked God to do is to allow you to have the Sabbath off.

Groaning, Cody replied, "Guess I'll see you in church."

Later, while laughing, my daughter telephoned and told me, "Cody is grumbling, 'I can't tell that ole lady no. I can tell you or my mom or my dad off—and yet, I can't tell that ole lady a simple 'No.' I know why she keeps asking me to go to church. She's trying to save my soul."

You guessed it, Cody!

JACK'S WALLET

LARRY AND GEORGIA were here from Kentucky visiting us, and Jack decided to go for his morning bicycle ride. When he came back, he was disturbed because he had lost his wallet. He had over $100 in his wallet and we could ill afford to lose that much.

We prayed about it, and then Larry drove our car while Jack showed him the area he had ridden. Georgia and I sat in the back seat looking out the window. Larry drove close to the gutter so we could watch the pavement over the area Jack had ridden his bicycle. At each little dark spot, Larry stopped the car, but it was never the wallet. It soon became evident we were not going to find it.

When we drove home feeling sad and feeling upset, we saw a man on a bicycle with a toddler in a small wagon hooked to the bicycle, in our driveway. We knew by sight all the neighbors, especially those who ride bicycles, and especially any with children; we had never seen him before.

He was in his late thirties, medium build, with a real sweet look to him.

He told us he had found Jack's wallet and was just going up to our door to return it. Jack was overjoyed and offered him a reward. He refused, saying, "I am well compensated by what I do," and with a smile, waved and rode off. We have never seen this man in our area again.

LAURIEANNE'S GUARDIAN ANGEL

JACK AND I LIVED in a lovely, large home with a swimming pool, and all the amenities of city life, when Jack decided to change careers, and become a real estate salesman. We drove through Illinois Valley once, and it was beautiful. A few trips to Oregon, and we found a two-story log house in the country, backing up to the Bureau of Land Management. It was at one time a summer resort, and our home was the one Gary Cooper, the movie actor, used as his hideout from Hollywood. Mr. Cooper put in a landing strip close to the log cabin, and Jack found it convenient to have an airport landing strip just a couple miles from our home* where he kept his airplane tied down. With the horse trails that wandered through our land, it made it a wonderful place to take LaurieAnne for afternoon walks.

When we moved to the log cabin, in O'Brien, Oregon, our daughter LaurieAnne was sixteen months old. My son, Larry, helped us move before he went into the army. Our sixteen-year-old daughter, Jeanie, was attending a boarding school about two hours from where we lived, and Jack had driven her back to school for the week.

It was our first winter in Oregon, and I felt as if I was freezing all the time. The cold, damp atmosphere just seemed to go right to my bones. My beautiful home in California was heated by gas, and all I had to do to get warm, was just adjust the thermostat on the wall to whatever temperature I wanted. In my new home, there was no wood stove, just a fireplace for heat, and if I didn't manage to keep the fire going, I shivered and shook for hours until I got it blazing again. For some reason, the dampness seemed to pervade my body. I could not stay warm, no matter how I dressed. To make matters worse, we arrived late in the year, and the only firewood Jack could buy was, green and did not burn well. When he built a fire and left for work, almost before he had driven away, the fire would spit and sputter and go out. It took all of my energy just to keep that fire going.

Our master bedroom was off the front room, and we kept our baby's crib in our bedroom. When I dressed LaurieAnne for her nap, I put her in sleeper blankets. Our bedroom was always cold. I read LaurieAnne a little story, rocked her to sleep and then carried her and put her to bed in her crib for her nap. I covered her with a baby quilt, and turned on the little electric heater under her crib. l turned it on low each day I put her down for her nap. This took the chill of the room. A glass of water in the bedroom froze; I knew without the little electric heater, she would be cold.

After I did the noon dishes, I went upstairs to change the sheets on our older daughter Jeanie's bed. While I was making her bed, I had the overwhelming feeling I needed to check on LaurieAnne. I shook the feeling off, because I had just put her down fifteen minutes before, and I continued making the bed. This time when I felt an even stronger urge to go see how LaurieAnne was, and I realized something was wrong. The feeling she was in danger became so strong, I ran downstairs, and threw open my bedroom door.

Smoke came drifting out of the bedroom. I was terrified I had disregarded my feeling too long, and ran to the crib, where I grabbed Laurie Anne and ran into the front room. She was breathing all right;

her color was fine, but I woke LaurieAnne up, just to make sure she was all right. This made her unhappy, and she started fussing because she was still sleepy, so I let her go back to sleep, and laid her on my sofa. I immediately ran back into the bedroom, where I reached under her bed and pulled out the smoking baby quilt.

After I yanked the quilt off the heater, and stomped on the smoldering part, I carried it outside. Coming back into the house, I opened the windows to let the smoke out of the room.

I realized that LaurieAnne had tossed the quilt off in her sleep, and when it fell down under her bed, part of it fell onto the heater.

When Jack returned home and realized how close he came to losing our precious baby daughter, he immediately ordered electrical baseboard and heating strips installed.

I don't know if it was my guardian angel or LaurieAnne's, but I know it was an angel that came and made my subconscious aware LaurieAnne was in danger. I always try to listen to this feeling; when I delay, I am usually sorry. I thank God for guardian angels, who never sleep, and I especially thank God for Laurie's and my guardian angels.

37

"God is our refuge and strength, a very present help in trouble."
Psalm 46:1

JACK'S VOICE

MY DAUGHTER, JEANIE, and I were getting ready to drive to California to visit my parents and siblings. We did the washing, I ironed all of Jack's shirts and clothes, as we were going to be gone for a week, and we cleaned the house. We packed our suitcases, along with a few toys for my youngest daughter, LaurieAnne, and told my husband, goodbye and headed south.

It was very late in the day by the time we left. I enjoyed driving at night, so I usually planned my trips where we would drive part of the night. I didn't take into consideration that it might rain.

We took the scenic road out of O'Brien, Oregon toward the coast, along the Smith River canyon. It was a windy mountain road. Many people did not know of its existence, and very few cars traveled on this road. Once we tipped over the summit, and drove through the tunnel, we were in steep, mountainous country.

The road had many curves and the slope to the river was very abrupt. I enjoyed driving this road, in the daylight where the scenery was breathe taking. At night, it was dangerous.

When it started throwing stinging shards of sleet against my windshield, I put on my headlights and wipers. LaurieAnne had fallen asleep in Jeanie's arms. I felt my stomach tighten up in knots, and found myself driving slower, as it was becoming difficult to see the road. We had not passed a car in over an hour, when around a curve, came a fast moving vehicle with headlights on high.

I found myself braking hard as I was afraid I would go over the side of the mountain, with those headlights blinding me. As soon as I hit the brakes, the car started hydroplaning, and then I was in deep trouble.

Losing all control of the car, we started skidding in a circle. I was terrified; Jeanie never said a word.

I heard my husband's voice in a forceful, compelling, way say, "Turn lose of the steering wheel!" and in a more urgent voice the second time, "Turn lose of the steering wheel now!"

Obeying immediately, I threw up my hands and held them away from the steering wheel.

At that second, the wheel started turning first one direction, then back, then around again, and this continued, while my hands stayed in the air. In a few moments, we were turned back around facing the highway in the direction we needed to go, without hitting the other car, or going over the bluff into Smith River.

When the steering wheel stopped turning, I put my hands back on it. Breathing a silent prayer of thanks, I resumed driving the car.

Jeanie quietly asked, "Mama, what happened? I thought we were going over the edge, and then when you threw your hands up in the air, I thought, "Mama has lost it; we are going to die."

"My guardian angel used Dad's voice, knowing I would respond to it. He told me to turn lose of the steering wheel, so I did."

"But Mama, how do you know when it is God speaking to you?"

"Jeanie, you have to listen to that still small voice, and learn to recognize it. Your angel can speak to you dressed as different people, or use different voices—but you have to pray and know when it is God. God knew I would react to your Dad's voice immediately, because your Dad always tries to take care of us."

LaurieAnne slept peacefully on, and Jeanie and I thanked God for once more taking care of us.

"The angel of the LORD encampeth round about them that fear him, and
delivereth them."
Psalm 34:7

THE HAND OF GOD

THE WINTER MY DAUGHTER, Jeanie, was eighteen, she decided she
wanted to go to Mexico. Thinking this was an excellent idea, I went
along with her plans. The one hitch we faced involved my husband
Jack. He had a one track mind, and at that time, it was consumed
with selling real estate. He was working seven days a week, bringing
home customers for me to entertain. Sometimes they stayed as long
as a week, while he flew them to remote ranches to show them
property. He thought nothing of working until midnight.

Jeanie and I knew if we were going to be successful it all depended
on our ability to persuade Jack to think about Mexico. We had to let
him think it was his idea. Jeanie bought Mexican tapes for music and
played them every time she saw her father come home from work.
The soft music playing very quiet in the background soothed his
nerves after working all day. She let them play all night upstairs in her

bedroom, where the music softly drifted down to our master bedroom. Jack heard Mexican music in his sleep. Her next ploy in setting the stage was to go to the library and borrow books on Mexico, which she scattered on the coffee table. We never mentioned Mexico in any of our conversations to him.

One evening he came home and asked, "How would you like to go to Mexico? I sold a big ranch, and my schedule is clear, but if we're going to do this, we need to go right away before I get busy."

Jeanie replied, "Oh, Papa, I would love that. I have never been to Mexico."

"Mona, would you like to go?"

"Of course. I have always wanted to go to Mexico."

"Pack up, then; we're leaving in the morning."

We weren't expecting this short notice, but Jeanie and I rushed around getting all the suitcases packed. My daughter, LaurieAnne, was two, and this meant packing a few toys for her. We were ready by the time Jack arose in the morning.

Before we left, we knelt and claimed the promise, "The angel of the Lord encampeth around about them that fear him, and delivereth them." Psalm 34:7.

When we arrived at the Mexican Border, Jack took longer than I expected getting our papers approved, so I climbed out of the car with LaurieAnne in my arms, and crossed over the border. When I saw a Mexican policeman approaching me, I went into a panic because I realized I had left my purse and identification in the car. Without saying a word to me, he reached over and took LaurieAnne out of my arms. I gulped, and followed him. He walked out into the middle of the freeway, and went back to directing traffic, holding my toddler in his arms. I felt completely bewildered. He didn't seem to speak any English, and my Spanish was in the same class as his English. Traffic rushed past us, as we stood in the middle of the road.

When he saw my tall, blond husband walk out of the building toward the car, he stopped all traffic, and walked back toward my car. I followed along in a trance. When we got back to my car, he kissed

LaurieAnne's chubby cheeks, stroked her blonde, curly hair and murmured "Muy bonita. Muy bonita." He handed her to me, and casually walked back and moved the signs halting all traffic. This was our introduction to Mexico.

I soon realized LaurieAnne was our greatest asset in Mexico. One old lady dressed in black, who was sitting on the street curb, was helped up by two young men. When they reached us, she stroked LaurieAnne's blonde, curly hair. She murmured, "Muy bonita." Wherever we went, the older generation wanted to stroke her hair.

As evening approached in central Mexico, we discovered there were no vacancies in any of the motels. Jack is a cautious man, and normally we found a motel before dark. Each town we came to, the answer was the same, no vacancy. The towns were few and far between, and we were driving after dark, on a narrow, curvy road.

LaurieAnne became restless and sleepy, so I traded places with Jeanie, and moved to the back seat to put my baby to sleep. They only had safety belts in the front seats of our new car. I heard Jeanie's and Jack's low voices as they visited, and the soothing sound began to lull me to sleep. As I started to doze, I heard a car speeding past us.

Jack commented, "I wonder what his hurry is?"

Jeanie asked, "What make of car is it?"

He replied, "Some foreign make I'm not familiar with."

Another whizzed by, and then another, and when the fourth car passed us, all new and the same make of car, Jack said, "I'm going to go faster, and keep up with them. I can use their tail lights to help guide me."

I thought I heard Jeanie's voice tell me, "Hold tight to the baby, we are going to stop fast."

I tightened my arms around her little body, and as I did, I was thrown against the back of the front seat, and slid onto the floor. My body cushioned LaurieAnne, who was not hurt. She landed on my stomach. My arm smarted from the friction of the front seat, but LaurieAnne continued to sleep.

Jack asked, "Are you or LaurieAnne hurt?"

"No, what happened?"

Our car was vibrating and seemed to be rocking sideways. Jack's voice held a note of awe as he replied, "I don't know. I stepped on the gas, but here we are sitting on the edge of a wide spot in the road, with the car out of gear. Someway, this car was picked up and we went sideways, and we're parked on the only wide spot. My foot is still on the gas pedal. This is impossible—absolutely impossible! We went sideways, as if a giant hand picked us up and moved us."

About this time, we heard another car go sailing through the dark past us. We heard crashing sounds and grinding metal in the sweeping curve ahead of us, as the car crashed into the car in front, and each car that followed crashed into the one ahead of him. The first car had stopped for some reason, and as each car went around the curve, we would hear another crash. Jack marveled we were sitting here safe and out of danger. We listened to the terrible wrecks taking place, and knew without the direct intervention of God, we would have been in the middle of all those cars.

Later when we worked our way around the seven damaged cars, Jack stopped and asked if we could help anyone.

"No, Senor. Gracias."

"What happened?"

"Senor, we are delivering these new cars from a distributor to a dealer. He was in a hurry to get them, and told us to move them pronto, so we decided to race and see who could get there first. I don't think anyone is seriously hurt, but Senor, you better go, because when the policia get here, they will arrest all of us and put us in jail, unless we run and hide. If you are here, you will be arrested, too. Gracias for wanting to help us, but you better leave."

He looked sad as he shook his head. "Senor, all seven cars are totaled. We will be in jail a long time if we don't run. Adios, Senor."

Jack thanked him for the warning, and climbed back into our car.

He asked, "How did LaurieAnne escape getting hurt?"

I answered, "Jeanie told me, 'We are going to stop fast, and to hold tight to the baby.'"

Jeanie said, "Momma, Papa said he was going to go faster! I had no idea we were going to stop. I didn't say anything."

Was it LaurieAnne's guardian angel? Or was it mine? Whose angel was it?

***

This happened forty years ago in Mexico, but I still smile as I think about it, and Thank God for his protection.

GOD'S HIGHWAY

JACK AND I MOVED to Cave Junction, Oregon, which has a small SDA church. When I commented there no activity for young people, I was promptly made youth leader. I enjoyed working on the programs for the group, and keeping the young people busy. I usually had one of them conduct, but I always was there. One of the first things I did was to re-establish sundown vespers on Friday night.

Jeanie, my oldest daughter, Laurie, my baby daughter, and I went to Sacramento, to visit relatives. We stayed too long visiting family and were heading home Friday about noon.

We stopped at a fruit stand near Yuba City, which was located at a triangle with another road. When we got back in the car, I inadvertently took the wrong road. About then, Jeanie remembered—we were supposed to be home for sundown vespers. I was upset. There simply was no way we could make it back in time. In those days, it quite often took eleven hours to make the drive from Sacramento to Cave Junction.

I was really disturbed to think that I had forgotten to return in time, but Laurie reminded me, "God can fix anything." We prayed and trusted in God.

We noticed there were no other cars on this smooth, freshly paved highway. When Jeanie commented on this, I felt apprehensive, "This must be a brand new highway that has not been opened to traffic yet. I hope I don't get a ticket, but I never noticed any barriers across the road."

I worried we might be going in the wrong direction, as I was seeing scenery I had never seen before. Jeanie reminded me that we had seen a sign that said "Yreka" when we first started, so at least we were going in the right direction. What puzzled me was there were no overpasses, no exits, and no highway marker signs. We were on a brand new super highway, with no way to get off!

Jeanie pointed out to Laurie the mountains around us were so different from anything we had ever seen. We saw lush pastures, fields of flowers, and magnificent trees. We passed rivers, and lakes. We seemed to be above most of the mountains, yet we were not afraid of dangerous curves, because we were driving on a straight highway, with absolutely no traffic. It was the most beautiful, serene trip we ever made. Jeanie and I were in awe of the scenery, and marveled that we were going to be one of the first to drive over this wonderful highway. I was able to keep the car at a smooth, seventy-five miles per hour.

I asked Jeanie to get out our map, and see when this highway was projected to open, as I had not heard of it. Jeanie laughingly commented, "Mama, I feel like we are in the *Twilight Zone*. No noise, no traffic, just peace and quiet."

Jeanie opened the map, studied it, and said, "Mama, this map doesn't show any highway that is projected to be built. I think Interstate 5 is the only one being worked on, and that is way to the west of us." So we relaxed, visited and enjoyed our wonderful ride. We found many subjects to talk about, but mostly we just pointed out beautiful things for Laurie to see. We felt we were seeing the country the way God had made it, before mankind made changes. We were in country that didn't show any sign of human habitation, just nature, unspoiled.

When we were close to Yreka, the highway slowly tapered down, to meet the completed portion of Interstate 5, and it seemed in no time we were home, in time for our sundown vespers.

When we bubbled with enthusiasm, telling Jack about this new highway we had discovered and what a short trip it was, he looked perplexed and said, "Honey, I haven't heard of any new highway being constructed. They are still working on Interstate 5."

Jack went to get his map, and we looked it over. I tried to draw an imaginary line for him, but he just shook his head and said, "If you hadn't called just before you left Sacramento, this would be hard to believe. There must be some secrecy about this highway because it is not on the map".

In about 3 weeks, we drove back to California, and Jack asked Jeanie and I to show him the highway, so we could take it to Sacramento and save all those hours. I could not find the highway out of Yreka. I felt confident it would be easier to find, coming from Sacramento, but when we started from the fruit stand, the road was entirely different, and no highway. It was a two-lane road, with crossings every few blocks. Jack drove this road for about 15 minutes, then decided there was no way this road could ever turn into a highway, and we were heading in the wrong direction. He turned back, until he could cross over to Highway 99.

This was over 35 years ago. This highway is still not on the map and is still not possible to find. The only conclusion Jeanie and I can come to, is God built a highway just for us, so we could get home in time to conduct sundown vespers, and to strengthen a little girl's belief that God can do anything.

"Angels who will do for you what you cannot do for yourself, are waiting for your cooperation."
Sons and Daughters of God Pg. 36

SAYING NO

WHEN WE LIVED in Bend, Oregon, it became necessary for me to have surgery. My husband, Jack, took me to Portland as he insisted he wanted the 'best doctor' for his wife. This was 165 miles from home, and we never considered it would be too far for him to visit me.

After the operation, Jack drove back to Bend to take care of our children, Jack Jr., age one, and LaurieAnne, who was seven.

My hospital room was filled with flowers sent by the different church members. Each day beautiful cards arrived from my wonderful church family. One elderly man wrote a beautiful poem about his love for me. His wife added a P.S. telling me she felt each and every word her husband wrote. The love pouring out in the poem by this beautiful, elderly couple made me cry.

My married daughter, Jeanie, telephoned each day. After talking to me on Wednesday, she drove down to my husband's real estate office, and tearfully said, "Papa, I think Mama is dying. I'm going to prayer meeting and ask them to pray for her."

Later, I learned at the prayer meeting they decided to hold hands in a circle and each person prayed just for me. This brought Heaven's angels rushing to my side.

My roommate turned on the television to watch Billy Graham. The sermon was on the ability to say no to harmful things. This pertained to things other than just drugs, alcohol and cigarettes. It was also about the ability to say no to drugs doctors might prescribe for you. If you knew they were harming your body, you must refuse until the doctor can change your prescription.

Was this a strange sermon? Perhaps, but I still remember it as if God had the sermon prepared and preached just for me.

The feeling of dying became stronger. With my strength fading, I fell into a semi-coma. Later in the evening, I heard a nurse call my name.

"Mona - Mona, you are highly allergic to the medication you are taking. Take these three pills. They will act as an antidote until the doctor can change your orders."

In a drugged state, I murmured, "Do I take all three at once?"

This was a foolish question, but I was not able to think clearly. The nurse didn't answer; she just walked to the foot of the bed and disappeared before my eyes.

Immediately after swallowing the pills, I could feel a change taking place in my body, which was still weak, but my mind was clearing.

The telephone rang, and it was my sister, Vesta Mansell, telephoning from Maryland. She told me, "Jeanie called to ask us to pray for you. I have, but I didn't even know you were in the hospital. How do you feel?"

"I did feel as if I was dying, but I'm better since a nurse told me I was allergic to the medication, and said the three white pills she gave me would act as an antidote until the doctor could see me and change my orders. After she gave me the pills, she just disappeared."

There was a long pause. My sister then asked in an odd voice, "Didn't you find it unusual the nurse disappeared before your eyes? What did this nurse look like? Mona, don't you know nurses are not allowed to give medication the doctor has not prescribed?"

"Her hair was blonde, worn in a pageboy style. Her eyes were blue, and she was about five feet tall. She wore a different uniform than the other nurses."

Vesta asked, "What was different about this uniform?"

"The sleeves were down to her wrists and the dress seemed to be loose. I wasn't sure how long it was, as I couldn't see clear to the floor, but I know it was longer than her knees."

This was the year nurses were wearing skirts above their knees and ultra short sleeves.

Vesta sputtered, "Mona, that was your guardian angel! I have worked in a hospital enough years to know no nurse would dare give you medicine without the doctor changing your orders. Don't take one more pill until you can see your doctor!"

I promised Vesta I wouldn't, but this was easier said than done.

The strangest thing happened next. I had read a wonderful book called *Ministry of Healing* two years earlier, and before my eyes, I could see two whole pages of the book. They were about healing with water, and how to get the poisons out of your system.

Drinking all my water and then dragging myself out of bed and bathing, I rang for more water. After drinking this, and taking another hot bath, I continued this until my system felt cleansed, and my mind clear.

The nurse came to give me my medicine and said, "Mrs. Barnes, here is your medication."

The first nurse called me, "Mona, Mona," the next nurse called me, "Mrs. Barnes."

"I can't take this. I'm allergic to it."

"What makes you think you're allergic?"

"A nurse told me."

"Which nurse?"

"The nurse in the long, white dress with long sleeves, and with golden hair down to her shoulders."

After explaining why I could not take the medicine, she became agitated. She immediately went for her supervisor. The supervisor browbeat me orally, telling me my life depended on taking the medicine, until finally I weakened and put the pills in my mouth. The feeling of betraying God became so strong that I spit them in the little sack by my bed. About an hour later, the nurse discovered this. She was furious.

"Don't you have any idea of the pain you're going to suffer from this operation? Do you want to die? You need the medicine to help dull the pain, and the antibiotic to keep the infection down."

Not knowing which medicine I was allergic to made me afraid to take even the pain pills.

She stormed out of the room and returned with her supervisor. This supervisor was very domineering, not used to having her authority flaunted. She ranted about the pain I was going to suffer with my stubbornness and stupidity. She left the room and came back parading nurses before me. "Is this the nurse who gave you the medicine?"

"No, I told you she wore long sleeves to her wrists. This nurse has short sleeves."

This infuriated her. She glared at me, "We do not have any nurses wearing long sleeves."

She went to the supervisor of another wing, and she brought her nurses, one by one. "Was it this nurse?"

"No."

"Was it this nurse?"

"No."

There were no nurses resembling the woman who gave me the pills. The supervisor became very frustrated. She finally told me, "I have brought every nurse on duty on this floor and you haven't recognized one of them."

On her way out, if she could have slammed the door, her body language told me she would have.

The next shift arrived, and I went through the same procedure with this nurse being upset because of my refusal. However, I was growing stronger by the hour. In my mind, I could hear Vesta's voice, "Mona, you know that was your guardian angel. She has come to your rescue more than once."

The night seemed to last forever, and I wished I could order a pain pill.

The shift changed again at 7 A.M. and my morning nurse came in cheerfully.

"Good Morning, Mrs. Barnes—here's your medicine."

"Good morning and thank you."

She bustled around the room, watering my plants and giving me fresh water to drink. She finally turned and looked at me.

"Are you going to take your medicine today?"

"No, thank you."

She gave a delighted laugh, and raised her arm in a victory signal. "I won the bet! I told them you would be stupid to take the medicine after the experience you had. A few of the nurses felt you would, as they have no religious background. I knew that was your guardian angel you saw, and I felt you would be foolish to listen to us and take the medicine."

She cheerfully pranced out of the room, telling me, "Everyone on the whole floor is talking about you and your experience. The nurses are telling all their patients."

Dr. Martin arrived, accompanied by two strange doctors. It seemed as if every nurse on the floor crowded in. The doctor sat down by my side, and said, "I understand you had quite an experience last night. Do you mind telling me about it, and why you feel you are allergic to the medicine I prescribed?"

It was early morning, and by then, I knew I was allergic. Lifting up the sheet, I exposed one leg. There was a solid red rash over every inch. Dr. Martin jumped up, and pulled the sheet down and my nightgown up, exposing my naked body to a roomful of strangers.

My whole body was one solid rash except for my face.

Dr. Martin exclaimed, "MY GOD! If she had weakened and taken one more pill, she would be dead! There is no way we could have gotten her to the ICU before she would have died of shock."

Trying to maintain some sort of modesty, I pulled the sheet back up over me. Dr. Martin went on to tell me my throat would have closed. He sat back down looking pale, and just stared at me. He remained speechless for several moments, with a bewildered look on his face.

When the other two doctors and the supervising nurse started asking questions, he pulled out of his shock, and became enthusiastic in answering them. They wanted to know what I was allergic to, and Dr. Martin explained I was highly allergic to the drug penicillin, and this was the worst case he had ever seen.

The other nurses slowly drifted back to their individual jobs, murmuring in low voices about the miracle they just witnessed.

Dr. Martin told me, "Mrs. Barnes, you are one lucky woman to have the guardian angel you do, and that she decided to intervene. I just hope my guardian angel is as dedicated."

I may not be rich, and I may not be famous, but God has always provided for me the things that are necessary, and without a doubt, I know God loves me. I am looking forward to meeting God and my Guardian Angel who has worked overtime taking care of me.

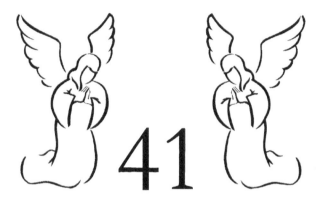

NEW VOCAL CORDS

My son, Jackie, was a little toddler, just learning to speak. One day, while I was cleaning my kitchen, and my husband was out selling real estate, I put the dishwasher soap in the dispenser. I closed and locked it and shut the door, when the telephone rang. Knowing I would not be able to hear on the telephone in the kitchen with the dishwasher running, I took the call in the bedroom. I had no idea my little one would know how to open the dishwasher door. After he opened the soap container, Jackie took some of the soap and ate it.

I knew something was wrong when he came into the bedroom with tears running down his face. I threw the phone down as he pointed to his mouth. Blood was coming out of his mouth where the lye soap touched his tongue. When I looked into his mouth, I could see little holes all over his tongue, in the roof of his mouth, and as far down his throat as I could see.

Grabbing him, I ran into the kitchen calling for LaurieAnne, my seven-year-old daughter.

"LaurieAnne, give him some water to drink, while I call the hospital for advice."

They told me to give him all the water I could get down his throat and rush him to the emergency room as fast as possible.

Jackie was not able to drink much water from the glass, so I told LaurieAnne, "Fix his baby bottles with water, and give him a bottle, while I get the car keys." We ran downstairs to my car, and I drove rapidly to the hospital. I prayed all the way.

When he drank one bottle, LaurieAnne handed him another bottle. We arrived at the emergency room, but the only doctor in the hospital had been drinking. He told me he couldn't take care of Jackie, or he would lose his license. He was visiting in the hospital, and he refused to step into the room. Standing outside the door of the emergency room, he called and told the nurses what to do, while waiting for the pediatrician.

When Dr. Moody arrived, he continued the process of giving him an emetic in the water to make him vomit. This procedure continued for hours. Jackie seemed to understand the seriousness of what was happening. He willingly drank water, and then vomited. Watching my baby vomiting was difficult to handle. It was a horrible procedure to watch, with tears running down his face from the pain. He knew we were trying to help him, and he never once protested this seemingly cruel treatment.

Dr. Moody told me, "I'll have to see him every week, to make sure the scar tissue doesn't grow across his throat, preventing him from breathing. I'm also putting him on cortisone."

This didn't reassure me very much, as just the week before when Dr. Moody was giving Jackie his baby shots he told me, "I only use cortisone when a life is at risk."

My baby lost his beautiful voice. He sounded like a frog croaking, all because I took my eyes off him for just a few minutes. Dr. Moody told me the best throat specialist in the state of Oregon was Dr. Scott, and it was advisable for me to take him to see this physician. When I saw Dr. Scott, I couldn't help thinking, *These doctors are getting younger every time I see one.*

Dr. Scott looked serious after peering down Jackie's throat with a light and a mirror. He suggested I take a look also, so I could see the growing scar tissue. I asked the doctor if he could cut the scar tissue away, as I did not like the looks of what I saw.

Dr. Scott told me, "No reputable doctor would operate on a child's throat, because it is too dangerous. You'll have to wait until he is at least eighteen years old, preferably twenty-one years old, so he will be aware of the seriousness of the operation. He would not be able to talk for weeks, and a child could not be quiet that long."

So my beautiful baby son grew up, learning to talk by whispering or croaking. We grew accustomed to his hoarse little whisper and consoled ourselves his whisper was attractive in an odd way. My sister, Vesta, told me, "Sis, when he grows up, the women are going to love that sexy sounding voice." I wanted to believe her.

One day when Jackie was three, his little voice rasped out, "Mommie, can God do anything?"

"Yes, Honey, God can do anything."

He went on playing with his toy car on the floor, and after a moment, he asked me, "Did God make me?"

"Yes, Jackie, God made you."

He continued playing with his car near where I was ironing.

"Did God make the whole world?"

"Yes, Jackie, God made the whole world."

I felt proud of him for his serious thinking about God.

"Does God love me as much as you do?"

"Oh, Honey, He loves you even more than I do. He died for you, so you can go to Heaven and live with Him."

"Then I'm going to ask God for new 'bocal' cords."

"Ohhh, Jackie, let's go sit in my rocking chair so Mommie can talk to you."

We went into the living room and while I rocked him, I told him, "Jesus gave each of us arms, legs, eyes, and vocal cords. If we lost an arm, or leg, or eye, or vocal cords, we will have to wait until Jesus comes again. When Jesus comes again, He'll give us new arms, legs, and vocal cords. There are some things we just have to wait until He comes again before we can have them. Honey, Dr. Scott said when you are a grown man, he will operate and give you a new voice at that time."

"I think if Jesus made me and He loves me, He will give me new 'bocal' cords now."

This concerned me, as I felt I had created a problem that might cause my child to lose his faith in God, when he didn't get the new 'bocal' cords he was praying for. Every night when he prayed, he asked God for new vocal cords, and every night I prayed Jackie would not lose his faith in Jesus when his prayer was not answered. My heart ached for my son, knowing he could not have this operation until he was in his late teens or early twenties.

Jackie continued to pray every night, and he was never discouraged, he just kept praying. He told me, "Jesus will give me new 'bocal' cords pretty soon."

During this period, my mother was in the hospital from a stroke, which paralyzed her, and my dad was in another hospital with terminal cancer. I felt God gave me almost more than I could handle, but God taught me a lesson.

On our way home from the hospital after visiting my mother, I stopped at a nursery to buy my daughter, Jeanie, and myself each a geranium plant to help lift our spirits. She and her three children always went with me to the hospital. Jack and I owned a station wagon, and Jeanie and I placed the plants in the back of the wagon. We were both feeling depressed after our visit at the hospital with my mother. We drove in silence, not talking, when I heard Jackie whimpering.

I asked my little grandson, Billy, who was one year younger then Jackie, "Billy, what is wrong with Jackie?"

"Jackie shoved geranium leaves up his nose, Grandma."

I turned the car around and asked myself, *What now, God? What more can happen?* We rushed him to the nose and throat specialist again. While Dr. Scott was retrieving the geranium leaves, Jackie bubbled with happiness talking about God and his new 'bocal' cords.

194

As we started out of his office, it dawned on the doctor and myself that Jackie was talking in a normal voice. My heart leaped with joy hearing his beautiful voice. I had been so worried about my parents that I hadn't even noticed his voice improving.

The doctor called him back to the chair and looked down his throat. With anger flashing in his eyes, he asked me, "Are you so vain you had to endanger your son's life? Only the finest surgeon in the world could have performed this surgery, and I want to know his name. I have never seen a finer operation, but he must have had no scruples to do this. I just can't believe any reputable doctor would endanger a child's life just for the money. Don't try to tell me he hasn't been operated on!"

Jackie continued chattering with happiness, as he said, "Jesus gave me new 'bocal' cords."

Dr. Scott insisted I look down Jackie's throat at the smooth line to prove he had been operated on, and I was thrilled at the miracle God performed because of a small child's faith. I also felt ashamed my faith was not as strong as my child's.

Dr. Scott continued to berate me for putting my little boy's life in danger, while Jackie continued with, "Jesus gave me new 'bocal' cords."

Dr. Scott turned to Jackie, and demanded, "Son, tell me about the operation you had on your throat. Where did you go to have it done, and do you know the name of the doctor?"

Jackie spoke up and said, "Dr. Scott, Mommie only lets you look down my throat, cause she knows you're the best throat doctor in Oregon."

I calmly said, "Dr. Scott, please listen to what Jackie is telling you."

Dr. Scott took a deep breath, and tried to be calm as he asked, "Jackie, how did you get these new vocal cords with absolutely no scar tissue? I know what your throat looked like before, and now there is just a fine, tiny line where the operation took place."

Jackie answered, "I didn't have an operation. I prayed to Jesus and

He gave me new 'bocal' cords.''

Dr. Scott looked shocked and stricken. He lost his beautiful, young wife to cancer, and became so embittered. I was told he no longer believed in God. Here was a young child telling him that after years of prayer, God performed this miracle.

Not long after, I heard that Dr. Scott came out of his depression, and was able to laugh again. Nine months later he remarried.

God hears all of our prayers. Sometimes He says yes, sometimes the answer is no, and sometimes, as in Jackie's case, later.

**

I believe the reason God did not answer my son's prayers immediately, was for Dr. Scott's benefit, so he would be able to renew his faith and love for God.

THE VISION

JACK AND I WERE BOTH ACTIVE in the Bend, Oregon church, where we were co-layactivity leaders. Jack was a ranch broker, showing huge, central Oregon ranches from his airplane and was so busy; I carried out most of the church plans we made.

We had an excellent business, a new home, yet we had this nagging feeling God wanted us somewhere else. We prayed about it each day and one day in prayer, I had a clear vision of a farmhouse in the country. I knew I would recognize it when the time came.

Returning from one of our searches in California, we followed the coastline and turned inland at Reedsport, Oregon. We drove through the tiny town of Elkton and when we crossed the Umpqua River at a wide spot in the road called Kellogg, I saw a narrow gravel road that ran parallel with the river.

I began to get excited, "Jack, turn down that road."

We drove about a mile and then I could see the farmhouse, set back from the road. I was beside myself, "This is the place, Jack! This is the place!"

Jack reluctantly commented, "There is no for sale sign in front."

"Jack, please drive up the driveway and ask if it is for sale. This is the place I saw!"

Jack turned into a private lane with stately oak trees on each side. We could see a large, two story farmhouse, a large barn, outbuildings and an orchard.

A young man came out to meet us and when Jack asked if the place was for sale, he said he only rented, but he believed the owner had gone to Sutherlin to list it with a real estate broker, and he gave us a name. Needless to say we hurried to Sutherlin.

We located the broker and when Jack inquired about the farm, the broker acknowledged he had the listing, but hadn't seen the place himself yet, and wasn't able to show it.

Jack said he was in real estate himself and if the broker would just show him the listing, he could make a decision from that. The broker reluctantly handed Jack the listing, and after a quick inspection—Jack pulled out his check book.

Jack was as happy as a clam. He and I had grown up on ranches as children and this had it all: twenty acres of river loam soil, fifty feet deep—abundant water—a fifty year old, large, two story, four bedroom farmhouse with a large, heatalator fireplace—a huge barn with a hay loft—chicken house—massive firewood storage building, a loft above with an outside stairway, for overflow guests—fuel storage shed—tractor shed--mature producing fruit trees—a long, entrance driveway, lined with massive oak trees and a white entrance gate—it just went on and on.

It needed some tender care, and for Jack this was a happy challenge. Our children and I loved it. The unbelievable part was the price. A member of a feuding family had just inherited it, and he wouldn't consider moving here because his family owned the farms on each side. He had defiantly listed it for twenty thousand dollars plus commission, rather than let them get it.

God's timing for us was perfect.

This was the beginning of the hippie movement, and it seemed as if most of the young Jewish rebels from New York City settled in our area. As time went by, our acquaintance with the hippies grew. They began calling Jack their "guru", and they came to visit and to consult Jack about goats, chickens, gardening, and food dryers.

When Jack had time he built his specially designed and patented, food dehydrators in the barn.

Our youngest son had an allergy to cow's milk and Jack was now milking, breeding, showing, and selling, registered Nubian goats.

Jack bought a tractor with a rotovator that prepared the loam soil perfectly, and he planted an immense, organic garden.

Jack double-checked to be sure no chemicals had been used on the soil in the last five years. We discovered a specialty market for organically grown produce and named our place, *Kellogg Organic Gardens*. I developed a following for my organic sauerkraut and brined dill pickles.

I am sure this is what attracted the hippies to us in the beginning. They were very health conscious—other than drugs.

We became part of their loosely associated group and were invited to birthday parties, and house warmings.

One couple decided to "legitimize" their relationship. They asked John, who had once studied for the Catholic priesthood, to perform the ceremony, and then they would record it at the county seat. I was not invited and felt hurt.

I was standing in the front room of John's home as they discussed the plans, and when he saw my face, he quietly said, "Mona, drugs are going to be flowing freely, and as much as we would love to have you attend, it would break our heart if there was a raid and you were arrested. Just think how that would affect your position in your church. You know we love you, and we are just trying to protect you."

This changed my hurt feelings to ones of gratitude, because I would have attended, not knowing there would be drugs used.

I met Alex and Diane through these hippies, who all lived near the tiny town of Elkton. Alex and Diane lived another 30 miles toward the coast from MY hippies.

I liked them both, but especially Alex. I felt he had great potential.

Alex was one of the handsomest young men I have ever known. He had a lovely smile and a charming personality and was very respectful. Diane was beautiful, sweet and lovely. I learned to like them so much that each time we drove to the coast, we stopped to visit with Diane and Alex; they had a little daughter, named Debbie, who always ran to greet us.

Diane soaked up everything I told her about God. She soon was asking me for more information about Jesus. Alex and Diane were both Jews who grew up in New York, and she didn't know anything about Jesus. She soon embraced Jesus as her Savior. I seemed to fill the place of Diane's mother, and she would tell me her troubles.

Diane told me, with a broken heart, that she did not know how much longer she could live with Alex, as he was a heroin addict. I felt stunned; all my life, I visualized heroin addicts as hard, tough, criminals. Not this charming and sweet young man. I asked her if she still loved him, and she told me she did, but with a daughter, she wanted a better life. She asked me what Ellen White said about divorce, and I promised I would look up all references to divorce and share it with her the next time I came to visit, but I begged her not to leave Alex until I could see her again. She asked me to pray for them, and of course, I agreed.

The next time I came, I brought Ellen White's counsels, and after we studied them together, she looked sad, and said, "I guess I have to pray for his soul and stay with him." We prayed together, and I went home.

When we stopped at her home after a day at the ocean, she told me Alex had gone cold turkey, and had not touched heroin in three months, but now he stayed drunk all the time and she didn't know which was worse. She had given her heart to Jesus, but wanted to protect her daughter from a drunken father. I was heartsick; it was hard for me to imagine Alex as a drunkard. She also told me Alex's parents had come to visit them, and how disappointed they were in their only son. I left some more religious literature, and after praying with her, we went home.

Several months later, I was impressed to take the book *Desire of Ages* with me to give to them. She happily greeted me, but said Alex would probably throw the book away; he was bitter since she had accepted Jesus. I had not seen Alex in some time, and was disappointed that I missed him again. No matter how angry he may have been at the world, he always greeted me with a hug and a kiss on the cheek, and made me feel as if I was his favorite aunt, if not his mother.

However, after she got through talking about Alex, I was apprehensive what he might be like when he saw me—when Diane quietly said, "Here is Alex now." She was worried he might throw the book away in a rage.

I told her that before he could do that, she should just casually mention that I must have left my book behind, and she thought they should return it to me the next time they saw me. I quickly put the book on top of her couch.

Alex walked in about then, and giving me a warm smile, he quickly hugged me, greeted me with a kiss, and shook Jack's hand. He let us know how happy he was to see us. We visited with him before we left for home.

We came home from Eugene one day, and on our gatepost, was a long note from Alex and Diane. Diane said that when Alex realized the book was mine, he picked it up, and casually started reading it. He stayed up all night, took the next day off from work, and read until he had finished it. He then got down on his knees and confessed his sins, and accepted Jesus as his Savior.

She went on to say that they looked for a Seventh Day Adventist Church near them, but the closest one was about eighty miles away, so they were attending a local church on Sunday.

Alex's parents had come to visit them again, and were so impressed with his clean living with no drugs or alcohol, they decided to be thankful their only son had given up his bad habits and accepted Jesus.

His parents bought them a new pickup and a new home in Eugene, and they would be moving. Alex wanted me to know that he loved me and thanked me for introducing him to Jesus.

I ran into their daughter, Debbie, several years later, and she seemed a happy teenager. She told me that she and her parents were active members in their church. I received the impression Debbie would prefer no one knew of her hippie background.

I felt strongly that God had additional plans for us here in this remote, rural location.

"For whom the Lord loveth he correcteth; even as a father the son in whom he delighteth."
Proverbs 3:12

GOD CHASTISES

WE HAD BEEN SENDING MONEY each month to Larry to help with his living expenses, and I had also signed a note his freshman year for a student loan. In addition, we had helped, from time to time, buying his books.

Jack had given Larry a new Toyota, so he and his family would have decent transportation through college.

We had just received a very hefty commission from Jack's largest ranch sale, and I called the bank for the payoff of the loan I had co-signed. I about had a heart attack when I found each year a new student loan had been added to the note I originally signed. Obviously there had been a miscommunication with my son and the bank when I was asked to co-sign.

I (we) now owed a very large sum of money, with Larry graduating from Pacific Union College. I asked if I could just pay one loan off at a time, and the banker told me, "No, Mrs. Barnes, the loans are all together and the money is applied on all loans. You may make payments, but the interest goes on, and whatever you pay will be applied to all of the loans".

I had already spent the commission money many ways in my mind. I had allocated the money for the original loan, but not this huge amount.

Now I could see all the commission going on this student loan I didn't know I owed.

I was driving the river road to Sutherlin, sputtering in my mind, "My daughter-in-law has all those lovely clothes, and I was still wearing a coat that was eight years old. It wasn't fair; I wanted a new coat too!"

Then God spoke. "Mona, why else dost thou think I have blessed thee?"

I was so shocked! My attitude changed immediately, and I felt humbled. Here God had blessed us so Larry could make it through college with a wife and two children, debt free, and He had to chastise me for what I should have done cheerfully and willingly. I felt immediate contrition and regret and I told God, "I am sorry! I will never resent any money spent on them again!"

I became joyful and continued on to town to pay the total off at once, feeling blessed that God had given us the means to help Larry become a minister.

When I told Jack that God had to scold me, and the money from the commission had to go to pay off this loan and not for the things we had planned, he didn't struggle over the disappearance of his large commission. He felt humble to think that God had used him in His plans.

Jack's next commission check was so large that, after paying tithe, we toured Europe with our children and a niece for six weeks.

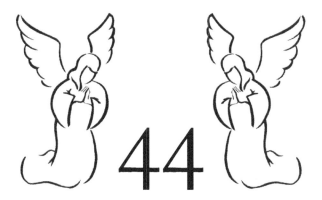

44

And it shall come to pass, that before they call, I will answer and while they are yet speaking I will hear.
Isaiah 65:24

DIGGER O'DELL

MY MOTHER HAD A STROKE, and my sisters flew in to help me take care of her. Vesta had flown in from Maryland, and Fernne from Texas.

We were in my station wagon, and visited with each other, on our way to Mercy Hospital in Roseburg, Oregon, to see our mother. I was driving, when suddenly I had a strange impulse, and pulled over and parked the car. My sister Fernne turned to me and asked, "Why are we parking here? I thought we were going to the hospital to see Mom?"

I replied, "I'll only be a few minutes. I have to go in that store." My sisters looked at me curiously, but I didn't attempt to make an explanation, as I didn't have one. I got out of the car, walked across the street, and into a Bible store.

The clerk came forward, asked if she could help me, and I replied, "No, I'm just waiting." She gave me a strange look, and then walked back behind the counter. I felt foolish, didn't know what I was doing here, and just stood in front of a book rack and stared at it. Periodically, I looked out the window at my two sisters, chatting in the car. I could not have moved if I wanted too—it was as if I was glued to the spot.

The door jangled as a well-dressed young woman came into the store, and the clerk again came forward and asked if she could help.

The young woman replied, "I want to buy the book, *Ministry of Healing*."

The clerk pleasantly and smoothly said, "We don't carry that book, but over here, we have a large selection of books on health where I know you will be able to find one to your liking."

I stepped forward, and said, "I can get you a copy of "Ministry of Healing" by tomorrow, if you care to give me your name and address."

The clerk gave me a disgusted look, and went back to her counter as the young lady wrote her name and address for me. I promised to see her the next day.

I walked back to my car, and my sisters commented, "You didn't buy anything—what did you have to go into that store for?"

I replied, "God wanted me there," and explained what happened.

After visiting Mom, we drove the 50 miles home to our farm, where I immediately started trying to find the book. I called my pastor, Elder George Reed, and his wife, Ernie answered and told me the only copy George had was on his desk, and she didn't dare give away his personnel copy. I telephoned the head elder and was given the same answer. I telephoned my dad, and he said the only copy he had was Mom's and he couldn't give hers away. I telephoned our colporteur, and his wife told me Floyd was in Portland, and she would tell him when he came home, but he didn't have any new ones, and only his personal copy. He could order me one, but it would be a week before they got it.

My family looked at me sympathetically and asked me what I was going to do now? I didn't know. I felt disturbed about not being able to find a copy. My own two copies had already been loaned out to the local hippies, who were trying to follow Ellen G. White's health message. I could not ask for my copies back, so I decided it was going to be up to God to supply the book.

Around 6 P.M. we were sitting in our front room, when I noticed a car driving down the country road, and then realized it had turned into our private lane to the farmhouse. A man stepped out of the car, and came hurriedly towards the front porch. He took the steps two at a time, opened our front door, and bounced in. I realized it was our colporteur, Floyd O'Dell, who we affectionately called "Digger." He tossed a book across the room into my lap, and dramatically said, "Here is the book you wanted, Mona. Now tell me the story behind it."

I exclaimed, "Oh, your wife told you I wanted this book."

He replied, "I haven't been home yet, or talked to her!"

I looked up in surprise, and asked, "How did you know I needed this book?"

Digger said, "I was at the Portland Conference for meetings, and when I was coming home, I found myself parking in front of a second hand book store. I wondered what I was doing there, but I climbed out of the car, and went in, and found myself walking towards the religion section. I stood in front of the books, and told myself, 'You sell these books brand new, why are you looking at these second hand books?' There were several of Ellen White's books among them and a voice told me, 'Mona needs *Ministry of Healing*—buy it.' So I did."

Coming home, I decided to bring you the book tomorrow, as I was hungry, tired, and I wanted to go home, but when I came to the overpass where I could either go straight home, or I could turn, drive 45 miles out of my way, and come through Drain to your house, I heard the voice say, "Mona needs this book tonight", so here I am, but first, why did I buy this book?"

I laughed and told Floyd the story of how God used both him and myself. The next day, my husband and I drove to Roseburg, took the book to this lovely lady, and had prayer with her. Then I gave her name and address to the Roseburg pastor, as my minister suggested I do, so they could follow up. We lived over 50 miles from where she lived.

I am going to look for her when Jesus comes to claim his own, and eagerly listen to her story.

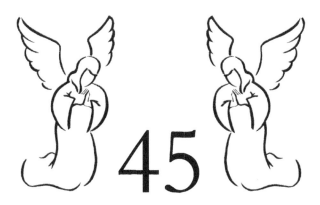

GEORGE I

THE SUN IS BEGINNING TO SET, and I am tired. My rocking chair looks good to me. As I sit and begin to rock, my mind drifts back to a hot summer day at our farm. I was working in my kitchen. Someone knocked on my door. When I opened it, a young boy who looked about sixteen, tentatively asked, "Are you Grandma?"

I looked at him in wonder, and my mind raced. Which grandchild could this possibly be? I was certain I had never seen him before.

He was six feet tall, had a nice build, brown hair, and brown eyes. I wondered if he could be my son's step-son. Larry had told me his stepson, George, had run away from his father and stepmother, his mother and Larry, both sets of his grandparents, and his aunts and uncles. They had no idea where he was. I hesitantly asked, "Are you George?"

He had no place else to run—so he showed up at the door of our farmhouse, and we inherited George.

Chuckling to myself, I remember how frustrated Jack became when he took George to town and bought him a new wardrobe of clothes for school. George insisted on all jeans, and refused any slacks or church clothes. Jack took it as a personal insult when George refused his offer of a haircut. They both came home angry. George liked his hair and his sideburns long, and Jack wanted it short. I felt hair length was a minor issue, and asked Jack to drop the subject.

I drove George to our local high school when school started and enrolled him. He was too handsome for his own good. The girls followed him in droves; the boys thought he was "cool."

Memories are coming thick and fast; going to football games at the small country high school, and cheering for him; my children, Laurie and Jackie, and I never missing a game. He was the star, and made touchdown after touchdown. He was so gifted athletically; he could leap up, grab the ball and change directions before he even hit the ground. He had the highest number of interceptions on the team and it was exhilarating watching him, as the crowd cheered him on. Jackie was so thrilled when George allowed him to wear his football shirt with the padding.

I remember praying for George.

My memories are acting like a movie now. Getting a phone call from one of his buddies telling me George decided to round up cows on a cattle drive, but neglected to get an excuse-note from me. The buddy said he heard rumors the principal planned to expel George. "Can you write an excuse note so George won't get kicked out?"

I wrote the excuse note and quickly drove to the high school. As I walked down the hall, I remember hearing the teachers chuckling, "Here comes George's excuse now. The principal is going to be livid! If she hadn't brought it, the principal was going to expel him."

The teachers loved George, but the principal was getting tired of his antics. I got there just in time.

He may be Larry's step-son, but it was like Larry was living at home again.

As I continue rocking in my La-z-boy chair, the sky turns a brilliant color around the clouds in the sky. Another memory surfaces of George drinking and wrecking my car. Rather than facing me, once more George ran away. I sat in my office telephoning long distance every person I knew, until I found someone who had seen him in a car, driving toward Drain, Oregon. Calling people in Drain, until someone knew of someone in Eugene, Oregon, and maybe George was there. Calling Eugene, Oregon, and telling that family George had to be home before dark, or else! No one asked me what I meant by "or else!"

I remember George coming in at dark, and asking, "Why do you care about me? I'm not even related to you."

I explained, "When you love someone, it is not like a faucet where you can turn it on and shut it off. My love will be there for you until the day I die."

I feel sad as I remember the bitter memory of finding out George was smoking pot with the hippies, and my going to their commune and telling my friends there that, if they valued my friendship and respected me at all, they would never give George pot again!

I also told them, "I want George home by sundown." They promised me they wouldn't ever give it to him again, and I believe they never did, and they made sure he was home by sundown.

Now I rock and dream and think about days of long ago, and how a stroke paralyzed my mother, so she then had to live in the rest home. My father was just diagnosed with terminal cancer, and somehow the burden of George seemed more then we could bear. My husband and I spent a lot of time on our knees praying.

I look at the changing sky, and remember the complete despair I felt after George was insolent to my husband, and we felt it was more than we could handle. We decided we needed to go to a motel for privacy to pray. I asked God, "Is this a burden Jack should carry? George is my husband's, step-son's, step-son. I'm asking a lot of my husband, God. Must we continue to work with George, when both Mom and Dad are dying?"

When we arrived home the next day, there was a note reading, "Dear Grandma and Pa, please forgive me." We realized this was the sign we had prayed for and God wanted us to keep him. We prayed for guidance and strength to see us through, and we continued to pray for George.

With my father fifty miles away from the farm in the hospital in Eugene, having another major surgery for cancer, I insisted on being with Dad, knowing my time with my father was not long. The snow and icy roads forced us to get a motel. When the storm was over and we were able to go home, we were in for a shock! What a homecoming we received. Our home was a complete shambles. George took advantage of the fact we were gone, and held a wild party. The chandelier was ripped from the ceiling and hanging by one wire. The refrigerator door was broken and hanging by one hinge. Beer bottles were everywhere, and the fireplace was full of cigarettes. My cooking utensils were thrown out on the lawn; the deep freeze had been raided. The lock on our one hundred gallon gas tank was broken, so they could all fill their cars up with free gas, and the neighbors were irate because of the noise. They lived a half mile from our farm!

We prayed some more! And again, we felt God wanted us to keep him, but life ceased to be quiet down on the farm.

The sky has dark clouds now, and yet the sun seems to be shining through some of the clouds. It is fascinating to watch. Slowly I rock, as my mind drifts to the night we received a telephone call at three in the morning. When the telephone rang, I sat up in bed worried, as I knew George was not home.

A policeman telephoned me from the hospital, and told me George was in juvenile detention. George was arrested for being drunk, for disorderly conduct, assault and battery on a policeman, minor in possession, open container in the car, a highway patrolman injured and in the hospital, and "inciting a riot." There were seven total charges, but the expression, "They threw the book at him," certainly applied. I couldn't help wonder, *How could a sixteen-year-old boy incite a riot?*

The policeman told me, "I'm afraid my buddies are so angry with my being hit by a car, they won't telephone you, and I can't sleep knowing a grandmother might be worrying about her grandson. The only thing I ask is, please don't go get him. Let him sit in detention over the weekend."

I agreed, but I think it was harder on me to let him stay in jail than it was for George.

We spent a lot of time praying for him.

My rocking slows down, as I dreamily remember the day while vacuuming in the front room, I received a mental picture of my refrigerator on the back porch, which I only used to store fresh vegetables. I just blinked the picture away, and went on vacuuming, getting ready for Sabbath. Again, another mental picture of the refrigerator appeared in my mind. I shut the vacuum off for a minute, and thinking, 'This is ridiculous,' turned the vacuum back on, and tried to finish, but this time the image came so strong, I knew God was actually telling me to go check the refrigerator.

Shutting off the vacuum cleaner, I went to my back porch and opened the refrigerator door. I quickly shut it again, and leaned against it, as I couldn't believe my eyes. It was full of beer. Not just a couple of six packs, but cases of beer! I opened the door again, and hoped I was just having a bad dream, but no, it was still there. How could George do this to me? I felt betrayed! I was always defending George to my husband when he would become irate. I could not telephone my husband for advice, because I knew he would say, "This kid has to go—this is the last straw!"

And yet, we had prayed for a sign if we should keep him with his disruptive ways. We also had two younger children to consider. We worried about his influence, but I felt strongly God had sent him to us for a special reason.

This time I was too emotionally upset to kneel in prayer. I went for a long walk—a lonely walk—down my quiet, country lane and poured out my heart, my troubles, my anguish and my thoughts to God. How could I deal with this problem of cases of beer in my refrigerator?

God gave me the answer. I went back to the house, backed the pickup to the back porch, and carted cases of beer to the pickup. I then drove twelve miles to the only store in the little town near us. They did not carry that brand of beer, and they were very glad to tell this furious grandmother they were innocent. They told me to drive another twenty miles toward the coast and that store did handle this brand. When I got there, they had already been warned I was on the warpath. They kept assuring me they did not sell the beer to George. I did not believe them, as I knew the mentality of the community very well. I commented on what measures I was going to take when I found the guilty party who bought the beer for him. They wanted me to know he must have had an adult buy it for him. I suggested, "I think you should buy it back from me and sell me root beer, orange, and squirt."

They were happy to. I drove back and carried the cases to my refrigerator where the beer had been. George was a very chagrined young man when he went to retrieve his beer for his party Saturday night and found soda pop.

When he came in the house, his face was red and angry, and I knew he had discovered his beer was missing. I told him as sweetly as I could, "George, can you imagine? Some stranger bought cases of beer and put them in my refrigerator? I know Grandpa didn't buy it, and I know you didn't, because you promised me you would never bring alcohol in my home, so I traded it for pop for the whole family to enjoy. I'm tired from all the packing of those cases of beer. Do you mind getting grandma a bottle of root beer?"

George later told me that he told his friends, "I don't stand a ghost of a chance around my grandmother. She is always one step ahead of me."

I wasn't one step ahead of him. God was. God always knew what George was going to do next, and helped me survive.

One day, George came to me with a request that he wanted me to pray for. He felt God would answer my prayers. I told him I would, providing he would read three chapters in the Bible each day for one week. He countered with three chapters for three days. I agreed. My prayers were answered when George started reading. He realized he didn't want to stop, and began reading the Bible more and more each day.

If only this meant a new George! I start rocking furiously as I remember what happened next.

GEORGE II

As I SAT ROCKING and reflecting on the past, Jack came into the room and asked me, "What are you thinking about?"

"Do you remember when George decided he didn't want to live with us anymore, and he came home with an older man? We didn't like that man's looks at all. He was hard looking."

Jack replied, "I remember. He asked for a full tank of gas, and money to eat on, as he was leaving to live with his uncle in Sacramento. We filled his gas tank, and gave him twenty dollars."

"But why did he decide to move again?"

"Just restless, I guess."

I continue to rock and watch the changing colors in the sky as the sun edged below the horizon. My mind continues to think about George and how peaceful it was at the farm without him. We had three weeks of quiet and no stress, before his uncle (who to this day, I have never met), telephoned me and said George ran away again, and he felt he was headed to Oregon. I thanked him. "I'll let you know if George comes here. What is your telephone number?"

Two days later, the feeling became strong that George was somewhere in Elkton, Oregon. When the feeling became stronger than I could handle, I left my real estate office, and drove to the local high school. I told a crowd of boys that I knew George was in Elkton and to pass the word to him that he had until twelve noon to see me, "or else!" They smirked, but I walked over to another group of boys and gave them the same message. When I drove back to Elkton, I noticed a cluster of girls, and stopped my car, and I repeated the message, "Tell George he has until twelve noon or else!"

Back at my office, I sat looking out of the window. I couldn't help but wonder, What will George's reaction be, when he gets my message?'

Soon I saw George across the street, walking with the high-school boys. I watched and prayed.

At two minutes to twelve, he strolled in, and commented, "Grandma, you wanted to see me?"

George came back home to live, and my knees were getting sore from praying for him.

As I rock, I look at the changing scenery of the setting sun. The colors are shifting; sometimes it is orange, purple or red, and there are still a few black clouds floating in the sky. Sighing, I think of what happened next.

I talked him into coming to church with me, and he wore his new jeans. There was a substitute teacher, a young man, who did not know George or his history. He took it upon himself to tell George that he was a disgrace, and showed God no respect by coming to church in jeans. George got up and left church, and hitchhiked the twenty-two miles home. He had no desire to go back to church, and I didn't blame him. When I went to look for him, the other young people who had been in the same class told me what happened. They were all sympathetic to George, and when I heard what had been said, I was really upset with the hidebound, arrogant teacher sitting in judgment!

How could I blame George when he decided he didn't want to

live with us? This time, he went to live with his mother and my son, his stepfather.

Watching the changing sky, I remember how once more my home was harmonious.

The tension was all gone, and peace reigned in our family. Then one night, around two-thirty in the morning, our telephone rang. It was my son, Larry. He said, "Mom, I wasn't going to call you, but after prayer, decided to do so. George decided he couldn't live with us any longer, and he is heading to Canada to find an aunt. However, he said, 'If Grandma was at the bus station, at three-forty-five in the morning, in Roseburg, he would take that as a sign from God that he was supposed to live with her.' Mom, it's your call. I wasn't going to tell you knowing how he's disrupted your life, but decided I should let you make the decision, not me."

Jack and I lay there stunned. Jack announced he was not going to drive forty-five miles in the middle of the night to get George. I prayed about it, and decided I had to go. Jack was very put out with me, as he didn't want me driving over the dangerous, twisty, river road in the dark. He also had no desire to have him back!

I was a little concerned when I got there, and found the bus station closed. I had to stand on the street corner in the dark, where the bus would stop—if there was anyone to get off. I couldn't help but think, 'I am tying a yellow ribbon round the old oak tree.'

When the bus stopped, I knew George saw me. He got off the bus, and I did not give him a warm greeting, but simply said, "George, we're going to Denny's to have coffee and a long talk. There's going to be new rules, and you have to abide by them."

We drove to Denny's Restaurant, and found a booth. I talked like a Dutch aunt and reminded him, "George, you're no longer welcome in your father's house, your mother's house, your grandparent's home, or your uncle's. I'm your last chance, and this is what I expect." He agreed to abide by my wishes.

George tried.

Looking at the changing sky as the colors begin to fade, I can't help but wonder if I should have handled the situation a little differently. Did I do the right thing?

I was in charge of the social activities of the church, and I decided to put on a bonfire social, down by the river; a bonfire for the adults, one for the young married couples, one for teenagers, one for juniors, and one for children. I had responsible adults attending each bonfire, and everyone was having a good time as they toasted marshmallows. They were testifying about their love for God, singing hymns, and I would go from group to group and stay for a few minutes, to make sure everything was the way it should be.

I invited George to attend, hoping the Christian young people might appeal to him and encourage him to come back to church. The pastor had preached a sermon about judging others and, usurping God's position when they did this. We do not have the right to judge others, so I was confident this time they would welcome him.

A feeling of disappointment swept over me, as I went from one bonfire to another. I really thought George would come, but just as I accepted the fact he once more had disappointed me, I heard the honking of horns and men whooping it up, as their cars started driving down to the river. A feeling of apprehension came over me, and I started walking up to the road. There were three carloads of drunk teenagers. I hurried up to intercept them, when I recognized George's voice. In a loud voice he greeted me, "Hi, Grandma, I invited my friends to join you."

I was in a quandary. I would have loved to have them all there, if they had been sober.

I knew these boys, and they were rambunctious sober—but drunk, they were unmanageable. George stood by the side of the car, weaving, and grinning. He was so happy, thinking he was pleasing me. I felt sick. How could I invite three carloads of drunken young people to a social group of young Christians?

I took the coward's way out. I told him, "George, I'm afraid your friends are too drunk and they might cause a scene. I don't know how to handle this many drunk young men."

He straightened up, and asked, "Grandma, what should I do? I promised them all a good time."

I could hear his friends, shouting in very loud voices, and their language was certainly not suitable for young children. I gave a quiet shudder as I heard them. When they came to my home, they never used this language around me.

I asked him, "Do you think they would settle for going to the drive-in show?"

He leaned back against the car for support, and said, "They don't care where I take them."

I gave him the money to take his friends to the show, and I prayed for their safety as none of them had any business driving. The mentality of this community surprised me. The parents did not object to their teenage sons drinking and driving.

As they drove away, I smiled as I remember thinking, *At least I'm making progress with George.*

Once more I quit rocking, and stare out of the window at the beautiful sky, with the changing colors in the west. The flaming colors were now fading. I felt sad as I thought about how disappointed I was when George dropped out of high school and what followed.

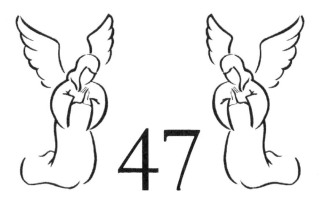

GEORGE III

THE COLOR HAS FADED from the evening sky, and I'm now looking out at streetlights coming on. I am still enjoying rocking in my chair, as I think about George.

Each summer my grandchildren arrived in swarms. Jack hired a live-in housekeeper to help me with all the children while I worked. On hot days, we took the children down to the river to swim. It was not a deep river. George always went swimming before we arrived. I thought he felt the grandchildren were a little infantile for him, as I noticed he would go and lay on the beach when I arrived with the children. Besides my children, Laurie and Jackie, there were the grandchildren: Tami, Troy, Toby, Larry, Georgett, and Billy.

I waded out to my waist and stood guard, watching them as they jumped and splashed.

I was not happy when I noticed my granddaughter, Tami, age 12, swim past me. My head swiveled to keep an eye on her, when I noticed she seemed to be going up and down. When her head came up the second time, I asked, "Tami, are you drowning?"

Her head nodded yes before she went down again.

I jumped down into the hole, pulled her out and shoved her back up on the ledge, where I knew she was safe. None of us knew there was a hole and it was around ten feet deep. As I tried to crawl out, George reached me and pulled me out. I realized he had been playing life guard the whole time, as he knew I was not a strong swimmer. George, with all of his problems, became an instant hero to all the grandchildren, and to me.

After this experience, I decided to drive the 100 miles round trip each day to take them for swimming lessons.

George decided he wanted to enter the Job Corps, and we were all for it. We drove him up the coast and were impressed with the beauty of the scenery and ail of the Job Corps facilities.

Every Wednesday night George called me collect, and he seemed very happy. This went on for several months, until one Wednesday he did not call. I became frantic.

Lying in my bed, I imaged all kinds of horrible things—car wrecks, a knife fight, being hurt on the job. When morning arrived, I telephoned the Job Corps and talked to the man in charge. He told me that George and two other teenagers went AWOL. I asked where the other two lived, and he gave me their addresses and telephone numbers. After praying, I telephoned Salem, Oregon where one of the young men lived, and talked to his mother. I told her I wanted George home by eight. I discovered by issuing ultimatums, George responded.

While we were waiting and praying, my husband and l talked about how we would handle this latest defiance of his. Jack asked, "Do you want to be the 'good guy' or the 'bad guy'?"

I answered, "You've played the tough role long enough, while I've been easy on him. I think this time, I'll be the bad guy. You can be the understanding parent."

When George walked in at eight p.m., Jack was calm. He said, "Your grandmother feels you've betrayed her."

I wouldn't speak to him for several hours. George appeared to be very sorry.

My nephew, Steve Mansell, and his childhood friend, Steve Koffman, were also living with us. When they graduated from high school, they drove across the United States from Maryland to Oregon. They wanted to live with us and attend college. Jack decided to take the three boys camping, while I got over my disappointment with George. The boys thought this was an excellent idea. While they sat around the campfire, Jack talked about his days in the Navy. This seemed to inspire George, and he decided to join the Navy. We heaved a sigh of relief. Before he left for the Navy, he sawed and chopped up a winter's supply of wood for us, showing he did love and care about us.

We decided with our two Steves to run the farm, we were going to take advantage of this opportunity, and enjoy a very needed and long vacation. We took a leisurely trip across the United States with our young son, Jack. Our daughter, LaurieAnne, was staying in Maryland with my sister, Vesta. It was time to bring LaurieAnne home.

On our way home from Maryland, I felt inspired to call the Navy Chaplain in San Diego, and ask him to talk to George. I had no idea how to get in touch with the Navy Chaplain. After we checked into our motel, I met Mrs. Lammerdine, a wonderful lady I knew before we moved to Oregon. We renewed our friendship.

I asked her, "Do you know the name or telephone number of a Navy Chaplain in San Diego? I want to talk to him about my grandson, George, and see if he can encourage him to go to church."

"I don't know it, but I'll call my pastor and see if he has it."

She telephoned seven pastors before she found one who could give her a chaplain's phone number. This pastor told her he was going out his door when the telephone rang. He said if she had waited just seconds later, she would have missed him. She felt that God had kept the pastor home just long enough to give her the telephone number.

She called me the next morning at six in the motel where I was staying. Now, six in the morning is early for me! I don't mind the midnight calls, but six? I was expecting to sleep late, and I was groggy. I also felt bewildered. Should I telephone the Chaplain that early? Jack told me to go for it, and so my long vigil began.

I smile as I remember what happened next. I placed a person-to-person call to Chaplain Morgan, and his wife answered. She said he was not home, and gave the operator a telephone number to call in San Diego. The operator rang that number and they gave us a telephone number in El Toro. El Toro Marine Base gave us a number in Los Angeles. Los Angeles gave us a number in Santa Barbara, and so it went. I can't recall all the cities we tried.

About nine in the morning, my hand felt numb and asleep, my ear hurt, and I was discouraged. I felt sorry for the operator who had been dialing Since about six. I told the operator, "Operator, cancel this call. I think I'll write a letter to the chaplain."

In a very reproving voice she asked me, "You're this close to winning a soul, and you're going to give up?"

This floored me! I felt chastised. I told her, "If you don't mind dialing numbers for hours, go ahead and I'll wait."

I settled back against the pillow, pulled the covers up to my chin, and settled in for a long session. However, on the very next call, the chaplain answered the telephone. He told me, "I'll ask George to come to prayer meeting next Wednesday."

I felt let down and said, "I was hoping you would ask him today."

He replied, "Ma'am, I have to preach today and I'm running late. I'll do the best I can."

I thanked him and hung up.

Looking out at the gathering dusk, I remember the feeling of disappointment flooding my soul, as I was expecting miracles by now. I later wondered if the switch board operator was an angel.

I felt discouraged all the way home to Oregon. We arrived home on Monday and in the mail Wednesday, there was a letter from George. It started,

Dear Grandma and Pa,

You will never guess what happened Saturday, but then I guess you know.

He went on to tell how he was confused, and he thought about the things I had taught him, but he didn't know what to do. He found a quiet corner in his dormitory and took his problem to God. He said, "God, I am so confused, and I want to please you. Please tell me what You want me to do. I want to change my life, but I am not sure how to do it. Amen."

As he stood up, the P.A. announced, "George Pagle, report to Chaplain Morgan at the chapel immediately."

George's response was, "Yes, God. Thank you, God."

The sun has set, it is dark outside, as I rock in my chair, and I am content. It was worth all the heartache and struggles. George, like Jonah, had quit running away. When he served his time in the Navy, he went to college. Jack bought him a new car as a present. He fulfilled our dreams, and George is now an ordained minister, working for God.

HARRY

ONE YEAR, JACK, Laurie, Jackie and my niece, Margie Mansell, toured Europe. While we were in Scotland, Jackie, Laurie and Margie got tired at looking at castles, so Jack and I took a tour by ourselves.

When we got back to the house we were staying in, the young people were laughing at themselves. They had decided to take a taxi home, after they hiked around Edinburgh, and when they stood on the corner to catch a taxi, none would stop for them.

Soon a group of men came out of the local pub and tried to pick the girls up. Laughing, but saying no thanks, they got a little worried as some of the men were very persistent.

A young man came out of the pub alone, realized what was going on, and said, "Move on, mates; these girls are waiting for me." The girls quickly agreed with the young man, as they felt safer with just one than the group. The men grumbled a bit, but moved on.

Harry, as his name was, then asked them if they were trying to catch a taxi and when they said, "Yes," he took them to the corner where the taxis stopped, and quickly had them in one. Before he let them go he asked where they were staying, and then invited all three of them to go sightseeing with him the next night. Harry came each afternoon for the three days we were there, taking the young people to places they would like to see.

A few months after we returned home a letter came from Harry saying he had arranged a flight and was coming to visit us.

When we picked him up in Portland, Oregon, he casually commented that he was an atheist. I laughed and said, "In this day and age, with so many miracles all around you, how can you say you don't believe in God?" Later I was shocked at myself for laughing at him.

So we all took turns telling him of some of the miracles in our lives. We told about how God loves us so much he has give us guardian angels and how they had protected us, and had saved us from harm and danger.

Harry was entranced with the idea that I thought he had a guardian angel to help protect him. He kept asking questions, so for the next two and a half hours we talked about our angels, whom God had given to each of us.

The next day, Harry and I went to the Pacific Ocean, as Laurie and Jackie both had to go to school. This time we discussed how God had created angels and how Lucifer had stirred up a rebellion in Heaven and caused a war, where a third were cast out of heaven.

Coming home from the ocean, I told him about the story of Creation and the Garden of Eden, and the down fall of Adam and Eve.

The next day, I drove him to Milo Academy to pick LaurieAnne up, and while driving to Milo, he started asking more questions about God, so this time I told him how God had made the Sabbath day and hallowed it and how the seventh day (Saturday) was to be a blessing to us.

We picked LaurieAnne up and I drove them to Crater Lake where he wanted to know about the State of the Dead, and he was relieved when he realized they were not up in heaven looking down and watching the mistakes we make.

That night he asked me about my library of books. He wanted to know who Ellen G. White was, and why I had rows of her books; in fact more of her books than any other author. After talking about her, I gave him the book *The Story of Redemption* to read, and to keep.

Harry commented to me that he had not seen any crime in our streets, like they believed in Scotland. I asked him what he meant. He replied, "In Scotland, we think you have crime every day right in plain sight in your streets." So I called our local police station and made arrangements with the Police Chief for them to show Harry what a normal day was like in the police department. I took Harry down to our local police station and they drove him around all day on all of their calls. Harry said that, when he got home, no one would believe he was treated this way in Sutherlin, Oregon, so I took his picture in the police car for him, to take home with him. I was later told the Police Chief ordered his men to wash their cars and have them in spic and span order. I think Harry was a little disappointed that the police calls were for a lady who locked herself out of her house, a cat that was up a tree and couldn't come down, and checking all the windows and doors on a house whose owner was on a vacation.

I sent him on a little errand to Hazel Squires. She was a lady in her nineties, and she telephoned and wanted to meet this young man from Scotland. She wrote a beautiful poem about him. When he came home, he asked me how she could look so young and be so alert. So I told him about our health message.

The next day, Harry asked about talking to God, and how you do it. He didn't know how to talk to someone he did not know, or could not see. He didn't even know the Lord's Prayer. I explained about just talking to God about every little thing you wanted to, like I did when we had worship, and how God always listened to us. He enjoyed having us come to him with even our tiniest little concerns, just like our Mother and Father did.

That night, I felt impressed to tell Harry he could take any or all of my books. I had read them all, and I felt they would do more good for someone to read them then to sit on my shelves.

The last morning before he left, he showed me his suitcase. He had thrown most of his clothes away, to make room for the books he wanted. He chose mostly books on evolution and creation, *Margie Asks Why*, *The Desire of Ages*, several of Ellen Whites, etc. He had a worried look on his face about his suitcase full of my books, and wanted to know if he had taken too many, but I gave him my blessing, and suggested he carry one of two more to read on his long flight back to Scotland. He looked so relieved and happy as he chose a couple more books. I told him he could have more if he wanted them, so he took out some more clothes and took several more books.

He asked me about faith, and I explained that if you had a grain of faith like the tiny mustard seed, God would hear and answer prayers. And all you had to do was ask God for more faith. Going up to Portland, to catch his airplane ride back home, Harry told me shyly he had sat up all night talking to God, and telling him he wanted to get acquainted with him.

I found out the name of the town where he was visiting next in Minnesota, and suggested he visit the local church there.

After we got home from Portland, seeing him off, I telephoned the church in Minnesota, and talked to the Elder there. I found out they met in a garage, and I was afraid Harry would never find it, but they promised to keep an eye out for him.

I learned later he did go to church, and was amazed how they rolled the red carpet out for him. They took him on a hayride, had him for dinner, and he was shocked at how wonderful they were—how friendly they were.

I telephoned Scotland, but got a cold reception from the pastor there. He really wasn't interested in contacting Harry. He felt it wouldn't be any use. One day, Harry called me and told me he couldn't be an Adventist there, as they were so cold. After my reception by the minister in Scotland, I believed him.

A year went by, and I didn't hear from him, then I got a letter from a Motorcycle Club in Scotland, with a check, saying that Harry had sold his motorcycle, and he had asked them to send me ten percent of the price, as he wanted to pay tithe. I turned this in to the Sutherlin Church, and for a mission story, told them usually we sent money out to foreign fields, and now we were getting money from Europe!

Harry applied for immigration to America, and I wrote to our Senator, putting it in writing that we were giving Harry half-interest in our business if he could come to Oregon. I was told we were not accepting any Europeans at this time, only Orientals.

Several years later, after we moved to California, my husband lost his eye in an accident at work, and it was doubtful the doctors could save his remaining eye. One day, while feeling in the depths of despair, I telephoned my church and talked to my pastor. I told him I needed help to drive my son to church school, as my husband had to have surgery on his eye, and I needed to stay at the hospital to comfort and encourage my husband, and I asked for prayer for us. Then from the bottom of my heart, I cried (and I don't know why!); I said, "I need someone like Harry to come help me."

Now why I thought that, I don't know, as the pastor didn't know whom I was talking about, and I had only seen Harry for that one short week about three years before. I looked out of my window and could hardly believe my eyes. There was Harry, ringing my doorbell. I shouted to Pastor Tilstra on the phone, "Here is Harry now!"

Pastor Tilstra telephoned me the next day, to see how things were, and told me that he never saw a prayer answered so fast.

Harry took over running my house. He drove our son Jack to school. He walked my dog. He bought groceries and refused to be reimbursed for any money he spent on either my son or myself. He drove me to the hospital in Oakland, Ca., to visit with my husband Jack. Harry expressed the desire to go visit some friends in San Francisco while I was at the hospital for all day, so I told him to go, and I would be ready to go home when visiting hours were over, around eight P.M., so he would have all day to visit and sightsee.

Harry did not get back when we expected him, and Jack started stewing that maybe he had been in a wreck, and should we call the police, as Harry was so dependable. I told him very positively Harry was not in an accident, just lost. Jack asked me how did I know this, and I told him I had no idea, but I knew he was just lost. I could feel it in my heart.

When Harry finally arrived, he looked frazzled and a bundle of nerves. He told us that he kept getting turned around, and he had crossed so many bridges, he hoped he would never see another one.

He had crossed the Golden Gate Bridge, and had to turn around, trying to find the "right" bridge. Then he crossed the San Rafael Bridge twice, and he was tired of putting out money crossing the bridges he did not want to cross. I laughed sympathetically with him, and kissed Jack goodbye. Harry asked me if I would drive as his nerves were frazzled, and I agreed. I was tired but I felt I was in better shape than Harry so we headed home to Sacramento.

I couldn't believe it when I realized I had turned the wrong direction and was approaching the San Francisco Bay Bridge. Harry wailed pitifully, "I can't face another bridge."

When I pulled up to the window, I laughingly handed the tollgate collector my $2.00. She asked me what I was laughing about, and I told her, "I was visiting my husband in the hospital, and I thought I was heading to Sacramento, not San Francisco."

She paused and looked away for a moment, then as if she had come to a momentous decision, she handed me back my money, and told me, "Just wait a moment. I am going to turn all the lights red on both sides and when it turns red, drive up to that point." She pointed the other way, where I should go. "Then make a U-turn, which will take you to the other side. I will have the traffic stopped there also, so you can then get in that first fast lane and go back to Sacramento."

After thanking her profusely, I proceeded to do this, while all the traffic came to a screeching halt, with all the lanes turned red, until we were safely in the fast lane going in the opposite direction. There were at least nineteen or twenty lanes on my side of the bridge going into San Francisco, and I don't know how many going the other way. For those few moments the Oakland Bay Bridge was mine. Harry commented, "No one in Scotland is going to believe that you stopped all the traffic on the San Francisco-Oakland Bay Bridge and made a U-turn."

I was not sure I quite believed it either! I knew once more my guardian angel was working overtime taking care of me.

Whenever I needed Harry, he was there and did it.

Finally the day came when my husband was home, and the crisis was past, and when Harry couldn't stay in the U.S. any longer. Because of immigration laws, he flew to Australia.

I wrote a letter to the SDA church in Sidney, Australia, and they took Harry into their hearts. One day, I got a letter telling me Harry had been baptized into the SDA Church. Later, a letter from Harry told me he had married the head elder's daughter.

Harry is now living for God. He still sends me photos of his three beautiful children. Although I have never seen Harry since he flew to Australia, I know I have a son in Harry, and we will be able to enjoy each other's company in Heaven.

CLINT

WHEN I DROPPED IN on my daughter Jeanie for a visit, her husband Bill greeted me facetiously by saying, "Dr. Barnes, I want you to look at Clint. What do you think is wrong with him?"

Clint was seven months old. I looked at the bulge in his groin and said, "Bill, I have never in my life seen anything like this. I think you better take Clint in to see Dr. Hall."

A few days later, Jeanie called to tell me Dr. Hall felt an operation was necessary. I needed to be with my daughter during this time, so I drove into Roseburg from our farm. Dr. Hall said Dr. Donahue would operate, and he would assist him.

During the surgery, Bill, Jeanie and I went to the chapel to pray. A lovely nun came into the room, put her arms around me, and prayed with us. When the surgery was over, the doctors came out, looking very serious. Dr. Hall had tears in his eyes. Dr. Donahue told us Clint only had a few months to live. He explained they did not know what he had, since they had never seen anything like it before. It looked like cancer but acted like tuberculosis. During the operation, the surgeons excised what appeared to be rotten flesh from his leg. They also opened up his abdomen and discovered feelers everywhere. The expression that bothered me was, "There was rotten flesh everywhere we operated."

Dr. Hall told us, "If the baby lives, he'll never be able to walk. His leg will flop, as we had to sever the muscles and tendons in his leg."

We were stunned and couldn't seem to grasp what he was telling us. We went back to the nursery, waiting for Clint to come out of recovery. I thought I was handling it alright until the nurse came hurrying in with his tiny body in her arms. I have never fainted in my life, but I must have turned white, as a nurse came rushing over to me, forced me into a chair, and shoved my head down between my legs. She told me, "Stay here, I don't have time for you to faint." It hurt seeing his little body wrapped up in bandages from the surgery.

Our church was having evangelistic meetings in Sutherlin, Oregon. Since my husband and I were both involved in the planning, we requested special prayers for Clint. For ten long nights we prayed for him. Clint appeared to get better during the night after our prayers. Later the next day, he would take a turn for the worse. We didn't know whether he would live or die.

I stood out on the church steps each evening waiting for Jeanie to bring me the latest word on how the baby was doing. When she arrived, with a choked voice and tears in her eyes, she would say, "Dr. Hall said there is no hope. He is dying."

She then returned to the hospital in Roseburg. Back into our church I would hurry to bring word to our pastor, and we renewed our prayers to God to save this precious baby. Each morning Jeanie telephoned me, "He is better." When evening arrived, the doctor's news again would be, "He is not going to make it."

This went on for ten long days and nights.

Our friends, Vic and Deanie McLinn, and Jack and I organized an around the clock prayer vigil for Clint at our church. We started at 9:30 a.m. Every fifteen minutes one set of prayer warriors relieved another interceding for Clint. Jack and I signed up for the late night slots.

We left our farmhouse at Kellogg and drove the twenty-two miles to church. We left a little early and were surprised to find sixteen people still praying. Some walked around praying quietly, others were praying out loud. What amazed me was the fact people were driving up to pray who had not signed up to participate. Soon the pastor's study was full, and men were out in the sanctuary praying. We felt so refreshed with our church family there, we stayed to pray for two hours. We felt close to God, and hated to go home, but Jack had goats to milk. A peace and calmness came into my soul, with the conviction God heard our pleas and Clint was healed.

In the morning when we arrived at the hospital, Bill and Jeanie greeted us with smiles. "Clint is healed and will live."

When we thanked Dr. Hall, he said, pointing towards heaven, "It wasn't me. The Surgeon Upstairs healed him."

Clint continued to get better each day, but we were admonished, "Remember he will never walk. We cut the tendons and muscles in his leg."

The doctors mailed tissue samples to ten different laboratories around the world, but they were not getting any results back. This was frustrating because without a diagnosis, they did not know how to treat our baby.

Picking up the telephone, I called my sister, Vesta Mansell, who lived in the Washington, D.C. area. I asked if she knew of someone who could pull some strings at Walter Reed Army Medical Center. This is where one of the samples was sent. We needed someone who could cut through some serious red tape. Dr. Maurice Reeder, Chief of the Department of Radiology at Walter Reed Army Medical Center, also worked on the side in the Radiology Department where Vesta worked. This man "ate red tape."

Vesta phoned back with the news that Clint had *tumoral calcinosis*, a rare disease.

When I telephoned Jeanie with the diagnosis, she was delighted to relay the news to Dr. Hall. He was stunned. He had not been able to get an answer back from any of the labs around the world, and now

Jeanie was telephoning him with the results, via our family relay system. Dr. Hall asked her, "How could your mother get this report, when I have telephoned Walter Reed Hospital daily?"

She laughed and said, "Dr. Hall, we are a large family, and it does have side benefits."

Both Dr. Hall and Dr. Donahue wrote Clint up in the medical journals. Dr. Hall carried the slides of Clint's x-rays around in his coat pocket, and pulled them out to show at every opportunity. Dr. Donahue took the x-rays to the next medical convention he attended. Clint became their poster boy.

Today, my grandson is a city policeman in Oregon, and has outrun his share of law breakers and arrested them. I thank God for answering our prayers.

TERROR ON THE UMPQUA

IT WAS MY PARENTS' fiftieth wedding anniversary, and our farm overflowed with laughing, happy, young people. Our children, grandchildren, nieces and nephews filled our home with their youthful exuberance. It was a hot Fourth of July, and the teenagers wanted to go swimming or rafting on the Umpqua River, at the back edge of our farm. It seemed the logical thing to allow them to go cool off by floating down the rapids. My sister, Vesta, and her husband, Don, supplied the rubber mattresses, and my husband, Jack, supplied inner tubes. The teenagers headed for the river. Don's parents were also visiting us, so we took lawn chairs to the beach for the four older grandparents to relax in, while they watched the little ones wade.

My swimming ability was limited, so I didn't feel comfortable in the river. Swimming across a pool and resting before going back is my speed, but I decided to watch the fun the young people were going to enjoy. We piled in Don's car and Jack's pickup and headed for the beginning of the river rapids to cool off. Watching the screaming teenagers float down the river was interesting. Later, Vesta and Don decided to go down the river without even an inner tube, and when they suggested we join them, I replied, "If I do, I'll go down on one of the air mattresses." It took a lot of courage before I felt brave enough to join the yelling teenagers. Watching all the fun everyone was having, I turned to my husband and said, "Jack, I think I'll go down the rapids, too."

"Are you sure, Honey? You know you've almost drowned several times. Remember the time you climbed on top of my head in the Caribbean?"

"Well, Jack—that was the ocean! My mask filled with water, and I couldn't breathe. This isn't the ocean! I think I'll be safe on the air mattress. After all, it is just floating down the river."

"Honey, I think I better go down with you. I'll hang on back and make sure you're safe." This sounded good to me.

We waded out into the river, and lying down on the mattress, with my husband holding onto the back and kicking with his feet, made me feel safe. Little did we realize after his back operation, he was stronger kicking on one side. Each time he kicked with his right leg, one side of the air mattress would rise in the air. Panicking I started yelling, "Turn me loose!" With his head in the water, he didn't hear me. The water was swift and we were moving very rapidly downstream. The third time he kicked, I flipped completely over. I'm not sure how I landed with my head in the opposite direction, where my legs were previously. My head was now under the mattress and facing south, and my legs north, with me gripping the mattress with both my legs and arms securely wrapped around it. I knew the only way of surviving was to cling tightly.

Jack started yelling, "Hang on, Honey—don't turn loose. I'm coming."

Jack's strong arms furiously stroked the water, trying to catch up with me, but the river was swifter. No matter how fast he swam, the current kept pulling me further away and farther down river, to deeper, more dangerous waters. I rapidly outdistanced him. My mattress was hurtling down the river, with my body under it, and my feet where my head should be. It seemed as if my back was scraping every rock in the river. Then my rump hit a large rock and the pain was excruciating. The rock fractured my tailbone. It felt as if half my body wanted to stay on the other side of the rock while the rest of me continued down the stream. It was terrifying, and my death grip became tighter. Flashes of all the advice I gave my children ran through my mind, and I realized how foolish it had been on my part in not going back to the farm for my life jacket.

When nearing the deep, quiet portion of the river, I began to wonder how it would be possible to ever get to shore, if I were lucky enough to survive. It was impossible to attempt to swim upside down under the air mattress. There was still no sign of Jack, and it was no time to think of turning loose.

As we swept into the deep, calm portion of the river, Vesta's two sons were treading water, waiting for that "crazy aunt of theirs," and they towed me to shore. Raising my head from time to time from under the mattress, it was with much happiness and gratitude I viewed these two strong, teenage boys. That day, Don Jr. and Steve became my heroes.

But I wonder—did they swim there to save my life, or were they just waiting for their turn on the next air mattress to come down the river?

***

Both Vesta and I feel brave as long as we are near our husbands.

51

IMPOSSIBLE, WE'RE SDAs

WE RECEIVED A LETTER from our son, Larry, asking us if we could find a house to rent, as he wanted to work for my husband, Jack, during the summer. He was our star real estate salesman before he decided God wanted him to be a minister. He was attending Pacific Union College.

The Lord was good to us! A rental came in with a complete inventory, and everything was furnished, including china, silverware, pots, and paintings on the wall. It was the one and only time this ever happened. A minister owned it and asked us to rent it for the summer. Larry and his family left Pacific Union College to live in the little town of Elkton, Oregon. All they needed to bring were their personal effects and clothes.

Jack decided to open a real estate office in Drain for Larry to sell real estate. Larry and I were a good team when Larry worked for us before. Jack found an office in an old business building. I was horrified when I saw the condition of the inside. It was necessary for major work to be done on the bathroom. Jack painted the inside, carpeted it, and overhauled the whole thing. It looked nice when he was finished.

When Larry arrived, he worked off the old listings Jack had, but immediately started building his own. I took the messages, arranged appointments for Larry, and tried to put property and prospective buyers together. I enjoyed matching personalities to houses.

One day, Larry came in with an open listing. The woman who owned the property had it listed with every real estate broker in the area. After Larry left the office to try to get another listing, a gentleman came in, and as he told me what he wanted, I mentally started going over our listings. I became enthused as I felt the last listing Larry brought in was made to order for this man. I told him that as soon as my son came in, Larry could take him out to show the house. Mr. Johnson had transferred to Drain, and was now working in this little town. He wanted to buy a house as soon as possible, so his family could join him.

When Larry came in, I told him about this new prospective buyer, and how I felt he would be interested in Mrs. Scott's property. Larry telephoned Mr. Johnson, made the appointment, and they took off to see it. Mr. Johnson said it was exactly what he wanted and put his down payment on the property.

Mrs. Scott was annoyed. She felt it should have taken Larry longer to sell it, and refused to pay his commission. She blew the sale. Jack took her to court to collect Larry's commission, as Larry needed it for his tuition at college. This was the one and only time Jack ever sued anyone for a commission, although he could have several other times.

A friend had written to Mrs. Scott, giving her Mr. Johnson's name, and suggested she look him up as they felt he might buy her home. Mr. Johnson also had been given her name and phone number, but neither one had contacted the other person. She said she had neglected to ever get around doing it, but her argument was that 'she had planned to.' She testified Larry wrote the listing at too cheap a price, the reason he sold it in one day.

We hired a lawyer, and Jack contacted the other real estate men in the area. They were willing and did testify in court in our favor. Mr. Gorski, the mayor of Drain, who also was a real estate broker, testified that he had her house listed for over a year, and at a CHEAPER price than she listed it with Larry, and he could not sell it. Mr. Miller, from the other real estate office, testified that he also had it listed for a year, at a CHEAPER price, and could not sell it.

When Larry testified in court I felt sick, as Mrs. Scott came to court with a neck brace on, and was portraying herself as a poor widow that these two ruthless real estate sharps had taken advantage of. I had never seen her wear the neck brace in town. Mentally groaning, I felt we were going to lose the case, as Mrs. Scott looked so defenseless and pathetic.

When Mrs. Scott got on the stand during the cross examination, she started testifying that Larry had harassed her. She went on to say Larry used obscene language, and coerced her into signing at a cheap price.

Mrs. Scott claimed that she asked Larry not to show the property on the weekends, as she wanted privacy, and Larry ignored her wishes and ran clients through her house all Saturday morning, while she was trying to watch her favorite TV shows.

I started seeing blood. How dare she say these horrible lies about my son? I was shaking so badly, it was hard to write, but I found a piece of paper in my purse, and wrote, *Impossible. We are SDA's,* on the paper. I was seething with indignation, as I stomped through the gate that kept the witnesses from the testifying area. Storming up to Larry's lawyer, I handed him the note. As I did this, everyone became quiet. The judge and the jurors watched me as I handed the note to Mr. Hill, our lawyer. Mr. Anderson, the other lawyer, craned his neck trying to see what was written. While silence reigned, I furiously stalked back to my seat.

Jack told me Mr. Hill was grinning from ear to ear after he read my note, then folded it and put it in his shirt pocket. Jack leaned over and whispered, "What in the world did you write on your note?" I told him. Jack whispered back, "I hope he knows SDA stands for Seventh-Day Adventist."

The questioning took a different direction. Mr. Hill took Mrs. Scott through a line of questioning as to what she had been watching when Larry interrupted her by bringing in the clients. "What were you watching Saturday morning? ... What time was it? ... How long did Mr. Smedley stay in your home, harassing you?"

When he got through, it sure sounded like Larry was a first-class heel. Then he asked Larry to come back to the stand for more questioning. Larry had no idea what I had written in my note to his lawyer.

This time, Mr. Hill asked Larry, "What do you do besides selling real estate?"

"I go to college."

"Where do you go to college?"

"I go to college in the bay area."

"Where in the bay area?"

"Near a little town called St. Helena."

When Larry said this, the judge started smiling. He knew what was coming. The Chief of Police also smiled, and so did the recorder.

"What is the name of your college?"

"Pacific Union College."

The smiles were growing larger on the judge's and the Chief's faces.

"What are you majoring in?"

"Theology."

At that the judge snickered, and the Chief laughed out loud.

Then came the clincher.

"What were you doing Saturday morning, July 21?"

"I was in church."

"What were you doing in church?"

"I was preaching the sermon."

The whole courtroom exploded into laughter. The judge threw his head back and roared, the Chief of Police held his tummy, and the

Clerk quit typing as she wiped her eyes. I am not sure what the jury thought, but when they came back, they turned in a verdict unanimously in favor of giving Larry his commission. My son was vindicated.

***

When the trial was over, and we were waiting for the jury's decision, the lawyer for Mrs. Scott came to Larry and apologized. He asked Larry for his forgiveness. He felt he had been harassing a man of God, and he looked sick. He explained he would never have taken the case, except she seemed so honest, as she told him how the real estate men had taken advantage of her. She said she was in a car wreck and was in terrible pain. She needed peace and quiet, and Larry was harassing her all day Saturday. He told Larry, "I would never have taken the case if I hadn't believed her."

Even though she had been ordered to pay Larry his commission, she refused to do so. What was interesting, later her lawyer ran for and became the District Attorney for Douglas County. He was still smarting from her lies, so when he became the District Attorney, he checked her records in every bank. When he finally discovered she had an account in a bank in the little town of Cottage Grove, he attached it and sent Larry a check which paid most of his commission. The District Attorney also put a lien on her property. This was good for seven years and she could not sell it without Larry receiving the rest of his commission. She was furious and told District Attorney he could not do this, as he was her lawyer. She sued the District Attorney for conflict of interest, and she lost the case. Larry never did receive the rest of his commission, but what he did receive helped with his college tuition. All names have been changed.

THE DAY GOD INSISTED

IT WAS A LOVELY SPRING DAY, so my husband, Jack, and I decided to have lunch on the patio of our favorite restaurant. After we were seated, I noticed a beautiful young woman sitting across from us. She looked classy and as if she had money. When her lunch was delivered to her, Jack and I both thought it looked so good that Jack leaned over and asked her what it was. She laughingly told him, "A fajita salad."

While we were waiting for our salad, the conviction came over me, "Comfort her. She has lost a child."

I pushed the thought down, telling myself, *How ridiculous; she is smiling and talking to Jack.*

Again came the message, "Comfort her. She has lost a child."

This message disturbed me, so instead of obeying, I mentally argued with myself.

I can't comfort her. There is no reason to think she has lost a child. Look at her—she is smiling at something Jack said.

Again the voice came clearly to my mind, "Comfort her. She has lost a child."

By now, I was really getting upset. I mentally told God, *If I go up to her and tell her I know she has lost a child, she will call the waiter to have me removed for bothering her.*

Again, the pressing thought, "Go comfort her. She has lost a child."

The voice was unrelenting, and I was miserable throughout my meal. How could I get up in front of complete strangers, approach another stranger, and tell her I know she lost a child? I squirmed. I resisted. I argued. I pleaded. But God's instruction remained the same.

"Go comfort her. She has lost a child."

Jack will think I have lost it. I can't do this, I thought.

I started marshaling new arguments. *Why should I think she that has lost a child? If I approach her and she hasn't, I would look like a complete fool. Jack will be embarrassed by my actions. What will I tell my family if she has not lost a child and the mental health people are called?*

Again the command, "Go comfort her. She has lost a child."

Jack paid our bill, and I hesitated. Jack gave me a quizzical look as he left, so I started to follow.

God whispered, "You will always be sorry if you don't obey me." Then louder, "Go comfort her."

This time, it was not a little thought crossing my mind, but a compelling, demanding voice.

I turned around slowly, and hesitantly approached the woman. When she looked up with a smile, I said, "God has told me you have lost a child."

She appeared startled, and I thought she looked at me as if I was from outer space.

I mentally said, *I told you so, God,* but I struggled on, while she continued to stare at me with this shocked look.

"I don't know if it was a boy or girl, but I know that you are grieving, and that God feels you have grieved long enough. You are making yourself ill. He wants you to know He loves you with all His heart. You are very special to Him."

She arose, threw herself into my arms, and started crying with deep, wrenching sobs.

As I held her in my arms, I noticed the other diners were averting their eyes. I stroked her hair and back, as if she were my precious daughter.

She told me between sobs, "My child was a boy. I thought God had forsaken me and didn't love me anymore."

God told me what to say, as I soothed and told her, "God wants you to know that if you are faithful to Him, when He comes again, your boy will be flown by his very own guardian angel and placed in your arms. You will be able to raise your son in Heaven where neither sickness nor evil could ever harm him. He will be raised the way God intended all His children to be raised. God feels your grief, and He hurts for you. He will be returning soon, and He wants you to be ready, so that He can place your son in your arms."

She sobbed and said, "I needed to hear this so much. I needed to know God still loved me. Oh, I needed this so much, just to know God has not forgotten me. I was getting desperate!"

When she had herself under control, I kissed her goodbye, and told her, "Never doubt again God's love for you."

As I got into the car with Jack, he asked, "What took so long?"

I sighed and said, "You'll never believe what I just did. I can hardly believe it, myself."

THE PAKISTANI WOMAN

STANDING IN LINE in the post office to mail a package, I overheard a woman berating another for being pregnant. "Haven't you heard of birth control? How dare you bring another baby into this world? What were you thinking of?"

My curiosity got the best of me as the tirade continued. I turned around and saw a very pregnant, young woman wearing clothing of the Muslim faith. She looked as if she would soon deliver. The loud-voiced woman was white skinned, wearing modern clothes, and acting in a condescending manner to the pregnant woman. My thoughts were sympathetic for this expectant mother, and I wondered how they could remain friends, with this type of sarcastic criticism. Completing my transaction, I started walking out of the post office, when I realized the young Muslim lady was following me. I held the door open for her. She pushed a stroller with a toddler in it, and she was holding the hand of a squirming little boy.

On an impulse, I turned and asked her if she knew the lady. Her reply stunned me. "No. I have never seen her before."

The unmitigated gall of the white lady boggled my mind. I couldn't imagine how anyone could have that kind of nerve to talk this way to a strange, young lady who was expecting a baby in a few months. Feeling sorry for her, I asked, "Are you alone?"

"Yes."

"Where's your husband?"

"I'm considered a high risk for having this baby, so I came home to have it, as I do not trust the hospitals in Pakistan. I must have my babies by C-section."

Now my motherly instinct took over. "Where's your mother?"

"She lives in Lodi, but she disowned me, because I refused to marry my very young, teenage cousin, so he could come to the United States. Instead I married a man I loved."

"Do you have any other family here?"

"No, I'm living in a motel and trying to make ends meet."

I walked over to our car and asked my husband, Jack, for twenty dollars. He pulled out his wallet and handed it to me. When I gave the money to the Pakistani woman, tears came to her eyes.

This was the beginning of my friendship with Aziz.

When I went to the motel she was living in, I was shocked. It was a small one room and bath, crammed with belongings for four people. It was also neat and clean. She told me she had a twin stroller floating around in the world somewhere, but was not able to get the airline to cooperate and locate it for her. She tried for a month, but they told her they couldn't find it or help her. I decided to try to help her, and asked for her claim ticket.

When I arrived home, I placed one long distance telephone call to the airline, and asked to speak to the supervisor in charge of baggage. I spent about forty-five minutes on the phone, applying pressure by threatening to take this to the newspaper if the airline didn't locate that stroller or buy the woman a new one. Finally the supervisor promised they would investigate immediately. The airline telephoned me every two hours with an update as to the location of the twin stroller. It had traveled to China, Japan, and was now located in Paris, but within three days they promised it would be delivered to her. They gave me an update steadily on the location of the 'traveling stroller.' I started dreading the phone calls. In three days, it was delivered to her motel. I soon became a 'substitute' mother to her and grandma to her little ones.

Aziz told me of her life in Pakistan, and the abuse her husband's family heaped on her. His brothers had beaten her while he was in prison for a drive-by shooting. When it came time for her to come to America, his visa was denied. In order to make sure she would try to bring him into the States, he sent his daughter by another wife with her. He kept her little four-year-old son to ensure her cooperation. She told me she discovered he only married her because of her citizenship.

Feeling confident our government would never allow a felon into our country, I tried to prepare her for never seeing this little boy again, unless she went to Pakistan. She swore she could never live there again under the conditions she was forced into. "I am an American, I was born here, and I do not have to live as a slave to his whole family."

Aziz told me many horror stories, and I felt torn about his even coming to the States. Aziz made plans for when her husband eventually arrived. He planned to bring another daughter by even another wife, as well as her little son. She thought if she waited until he felt he had control over her, and went visiting his cousins in a town near us, she could escape with her four children. She wanted to get as far away from him as possible. His two prior wives divorced him, but he had custody of their daughters.

Our county found a two-bedroom home for her, and her living conditions improved.

Soon our county moved her family into a large three-bedroom home. Aziz took in sewing to help supplement the money she received.

I found myself buying toys for the little boys, and even clothes. When I realized she liked to read and had no reading material, I took her one of my Christian books by Max Lucado, and my copy of the Koran. When I handed her the Koran, she kissed it, and said, "Oh, thank you so much. Thank you so much." She read Max Lucado's book completely through and asked for another book.

Taking presents to the little children delighted me. I called the two boys Jesse and Billy, as I could not pronounce their names. Aziz was worried about Billy, as the doctor told her he was diagnosed as having development problems because he didn't talk. He was only a fourteen-month-old toddler. I felt it was the shock of moving from a country where he spoke one language and moving to a country where he did not understand English.

When Christmas came, I could not bear the thought of the children without presents, so Jack and I bought gifts for the family. When Billy opened his present, the little toddler recognized his toy immediately as Barney. He rushed to my side babbling, "Barney, Barney, Barney." He hugged Barney to his chest, and kissed it. I felt a rush of warmth go through my body, and told his mother, "I'm not worried about his learning to talk. Just listen to him."

She enrolled the oldest boy in kindergarten under the name of Jesse.

Her doctor scheduled her for the C-section the same day the baby was due. I felt this was cutting it very thin! When she telephoned me she was in labor, my husband, Jack, drove me to the hospital. I thought I would be left out in the room where Jack was, but I found myself being suited up, and brought into the operating room. It was an experience I never even dreamed I would ever be able to witness.

The doctor giving the anesthesia was unhappy. He kept checking in every fifteen minutes with me, but her physician was not there. The nurses had everything ready for the operation, and were expressing displeasure with the doctor, and what they thought of him. The anesthesiologist finally told me, "I have other operations scheduled, and I'm sorry, but if he isn't here in another ten minutes, I have to leave for another operation." Soon, he left and took care of the other operation, and when he came back, her doctor still had not arrived.

This worried me, watching Aziz in heavy labor, and knowing she could not dilate for some reason. I couldn't help wondering if the reason the doctor was so nonchalant about her care had to do with her being a welfare case or her nationality. There was no necessity in Aziz having to go into hard labor, knowing the baby could not be delivered. She should have been scheduled at least a couple of days before the due date. I became furious with him, as I watched Aziz suffer. I talked to her in a low, comforting voice as I kept wiping the sweat off her face.

When her doctor strolled in two hours late for the scheduled C-section, he gave no explanation as to why he arrived so late. Things moved fast once the doctor arrived. He told me, "Stand at her head, and wipe the sweat off and keep her calm."

This I was already attempting to do, and thought, *He's not very observant, if he can't see me doing this.*

When she was cut open, the doctor in a very calm voice said, "There's a cord around the neck."

He flipped the cord off. "Second cord around the neck." Again, he flipped the second cord away.

Looking on, I could still see a cord around this precious baby's neck. The doctor again in a calm voice stated, "Third cord around the neck," and flipped it away.

Within a few seconds the baby was removed, weighed, and wrapped in a blanket and placed in my arms. The nurse said, "Grandma, take her to the nursery."

A nurse ran ahead of me, leading the way, while I carried the newest United States citizen. Things changed rapidly when I entered the nursery. The nurse said, "Scrub up for five to six minutes," as she took the baby away from me. I scrubbed my arms, and thought, *This is strange. No one had me scrub up in the operating room, where they cut her open.*

After I was scrubbed up to the nurse's satisfaction, the baby again was placed in my arms, and I was told to rock her. What a wonderful, satisfying feeling to hold and rock a brand-new baby in my arms at the age of eighty.

I continued to be a 'mother' and 'grandmother' for the next year to this lovely family, until her husband in Pakistan gained his visa, and moved to California. I saw Aziz once after her husband arrived. When I telephoned her, I found the telephone disconnected, and I have not heard from her since. I hope Aziz made good on her escape from this abusive relationship. I may never see her again, but I feel blessed that I was able to be at the birth of a new baby, and help Aziz through a difficult time of her life.

THE STILL SMALL VOICE

OUR SON, JACK, decided to move back to his birthplace, he went on a crusade to persuade family members to return to Oregon. He felt nothing was holding him to the Sacramento area except immediate family.

Jack and his wife, Ellen, made several trips to Oregon before they found their 'dream home.' On Jack's second trip, he looked for a home for his parents. He found one overlooking the Umpqua River, with three bedrooms and two baths, and closed the deal for both homes. Jack convinced his sister, LaurieAnne, to come and she decided to move the next year, after her son, Austin, graduated from high school.

Soon we noticed Jack's friends were selling and moving to Oregon, some from out of state. It looked like he was developing a compound of families who wanted to be near him. Forbes magazine named him the number one amateur stock picker for the year 2005, and his friends wanted his advice.

My husband decided he wanted to return to Oregon, as the highways in California were dangerous for a driver with only one eye.

I told him I felt we needed to pray about it. Each time we prayed, I heard this still, small voice, "Harold will need you."

This puzzled me. I love my oldest son, Harold, but I could not see how he might need me. He is a millionaire. His children are all grown with children of their own. Jack's babies are two and three, and I wanted to be near these grandchildren.

Harold has been involved with car racing for forty years as a hobby, and when he retired from the racing aspects, he became an official at the track. He lives close by and drops in several times a week. Twice when I became ill, he rushed me to the hospital and sat in the waiting room of the E.R. until 4:00 AM., until they finally decided to admit me. He is a wonderful son, but I could not imagine any way he might need me. Yet, each time I prayed, I heard the words very clearly in my mind, "Harold will need you."

His wife, Randy, invites us to their home every time they entertain his children, and she always serves a catered meal. Usually, once or twice a year, they take me out to see a musical or play. They give us tickets to the River Cat's baseball games. It is wonderful to be the recipient of all of these generous, wonderful gifts, but it seemed impossible to conceive how he might possibly ever need *me*. I am in my eighties.

Randy's only living relatives are one daughter and three grand babies. She inherited a large sum of money when her mother died, but she lost her emotional support system. As a bank president, she is the epitome of a businesswoman.

After I repeatedly heard these words, "Harold will need you," we reluctantly decided not to move to Oregon. Our son, Jack, became unhappy with our decision; however, he kept the home on the river for a guesthouse and office. His guesthouse is occupied steadily, and this turned out to be a blessing for his wife, Ellen. Relatives and friends enjoy visiting Jack, and have a home at their disposal.

A few months later, I received the telephone call all parents dread.

"Hal has been hit at the track by a car going more than fifty miles an hour. If you want to see him alive, you better come to Marysville as fast as you can."

My daughter, LaurieAnne, immediately drove me to Marysville where we checked into a motel and stayed for three days, until he was out of immediate danger.

Harold was standing on a curve at the racetrack, when a car, whose steering gear broke, hit him. This threw him up in the air. When Harold came down, he was hit again, and then dragged until the car hit a steel post. This pinned my son under the car. His left hip was shattered, and his right leg broken from the hip down to his ankle.

Harold is home now, and at least three times a week, I "son-sit," so his wife can buy things she needs—groceries or medical supplies. He is not able to put his legs on the ground, so this means each time he gets tired of sitting in one position, I take his ankles and move his legs, as he shifts his body with his arms, and with a board, slides to the new position. We do, this every fifteen minutes, from the sofa, to the wheelchair, back to the sofa.

Harold will not be able to walk normally for another year and half, so he will need me for some time. I go home exhausted, and sleep late the next day. My husband will not wake me for any telephone calls, and as my sister Vesta told me when she calls, Jack will say, "Your sister is sleeping. She is tired."

I never dreamed this son would ever need me, but I am so glad that I once more listened to this still, small voice.

JODY'S WEDDING RECEPTION

ONE SABBATH MORNING, while my husband, Jack, and I were sitting in church, LaurieAnne, our daughter, noticed a young man sitting across the church by himself. When it came time to welcome the visitors with a neighborly handshake, no one greeted him. LaurieAnne nudged me.

"Mom, no one is shaking his hand. Go and greet him. Why don't you go and give him your mother's hug and make him feel welcome?"

I went over to the young man. He had long, dark hair that hung below his shoulders. He had on a tank top and shorts, and wore thongs on his feet. He was still sitting, arms folded firmly in an attitude of defiance, when I reached him. I took his hand down to shake it, and smiled.

"Good morning. I'm so happy you came to church today, and I want you to know God loves you."

The young man looked shocked, and said nothing. Still smiling, I turned and went back to my seat.

The next Sabbath, the young man returned and sat by himself in the same church pew. Again, no one greeted him. I walked across the church toward him. This time, I not only took his hand down to shake, but leaned forward, and kissed him on the cheek and said, "I want you to know God loves you and so do I. Do you mind telling me your name, so I'll know how to pray for you?"

He looked stunned, and then quietly told me, "My name is Jody."

I continued to greet him in this fashion for several months, and then my husband and I moved to another church.

A few years went by, and we decided to visit our old church. After the sermon, as we were leaving, I noticed two ministers standing by the other door. As we walked away, I heard Jody's familiar voice ask, "Mona, don't I get my kiss?"

Whirling around, I looked for the voice. I didn't see him anywhere, and then glancing in the direction of the two ministers, I noticed both were smiling. The youngest of the two was standing with a Bible in his hands. My eyes widened and I asked, "Jody?"

He opened his arms, and I ran into them for a hug and a kiss on my cheek. Then he asked, "Do you love me more with my short hair, or with my long hair?"

I replied, "When I looked into your eyes years ago and told you I loved you, I meant it. It doesn't matter to me if your hair is long or short."

Three or four more years went by, and I hadn't seen or heard from him. Rumors reached me he was now a minister back East. One night I awoke out of a sound sleep, and distinctly heard the words, "Pray for Jody."

Waking Jack, I said, "Honey, I don't know why, but we have to pray for Jody."

"Jody who?" he asked.

"Remember the young man with the long hair I pointed out to you in church several years ago?"

Jack remembered him. We both prayed, and then we drifted back to sleep.

After that and occasionally during the day, I would hear the words, "Pray for Jody." Jack became used to my coming into our computer room and saying, "We have to pray for Jody. I have no idea why, but we need to pray." The command to pray for Jody continued for about six months.

One day we were surprised to receive our first letter from Jody asking if I remembered him. I answered and let him know we were praying for him. He said his health had become very precarious, and he asked for our prayers. I assured him we would continue praying for him. Jody gave me his telephone number and we began speaking frequently, when he phoned for what he called a "mother's advice."

At such times, I wondered, *How is a lay person supposed to give a minister advice?*

When I prayed, God assured me He gave me words of wisdom when Larry, my son, who is a minister, asked me for counsel. As time passed, we grew to love Jody as a grandson.

When he was ordained to the ministry, he made arrangements for me to fly back to Pennsylvania, but because of an illness, I was unable to attend. Later, when Jody married, he made plans to help me with the finances to fly back, and was reserving a motel room for me. I accepted the invitation and looked forward to attending his wedding. But because of my age, and flying alone, my children convinced me it was the better part of wisdom not to attend. I tearfully acquiesced to their reasons.

Jody told me he was going to Hawaii for his honeymoon, but would be in California after their honeymoon, and he and Lisa, his bride, would be able to visit us for a few hours before they flew back to Pennsylvania.

Laurie telephoned Jody and said, "When you come back from your honeymoon in Hawaii, we'd like to have a reception here for you, so Mom can feel she at least had a small part in your wedding."

Laurie thought the reception could be held in our home, but when I talked to Jody, I realized my house would not be big enough, and decided to ask our church board about having it in our West Sacramento church. However, when I again phoned Jody, he said,

"We will need a reception hall large enough to hold around 100 people. I can't invite some of my family and leave others out."

I replied, "Laurie was married in her brother's backyard, because there were more guests than would fit in our West Sacramento church, and we couldn't afford to pay what the larger churches charged to non-members."

"Well, in that case," Jody said sadly, "I'll pare the list down."

While making the arrangements for the reception, I decided to phone the Woodside church, where we used to hold our membership, and asked, "Can I reserve your reception hall, if this is possible, and how much would it cost?"

The church remembered our family, and recalled Jody, when he was baptized there. I had no idea he had been baptized there. The next day, I received a phone call from the church, saying the church board voted it would be a Christmas present to both Jody and me. This solved this problem. It was large enough to hold Jody's family and guests.

My friend, Rita Torrez, helped by providing the table clothes, the knife to cut the wedding cake, silver candlestick holders to put on all the tables, and other necessary items. Laurie drove me to the bakery to pick out the cake, then to the store to buy apple cider, peppermints and nuts for refreshments. Laurie also decided on what should be engraved on the invitations.

A problem now arose. I only received the names and addresses of Jody's family by e-mail on Sunday morning, a week before the reception. He was leaving Pennsylvania for Hawaii for his honeymoon on Sunday, and would arrive in Sacramento from Hawaii for our reception for him on Friday. This gave me five days to pull the loose ends together.

We mailed the invitations out on Tuesday. On Thursday, Laurie, Rita, and I decorated the reception hall. We were not able to finish the job before we had to lock up their reception hall. Coming home exhausted, I sat in my La-z-boy recliner, discouraged. I knew, mailing the invitations out so late, that the guests would have no time to respond, and I had no idea how many refreshments to buy. *And How,* I worried, *am I going to have the energy to finish the decorating Saturday after sundown, before the guests arrive? Will I have enough apple cider and cake?*

Shutting my eyes, I started talking to God, asking how I was going to manage this celebration when I was so tired.

God, I've bitten off more than I can chew. I'm eighty-one now, and I don't have the energy level I once had. What if we run out of hot apple cider? Dear Father, I pleaded, I *think I have made a big mistake in agreeing to undertake this reception. I'm so afraid I won't have enough cider.*

My eyes were closed, when I heard a voice command, "Look up!"

When I looked, a very tall man with a smiling face was standing by my china cabinet.

He was at least six feet seven inches tall. He wore dress slacks, and a sweater. I was not terrified in the least by his presence. Warmth and peace filled my heart and mind. Although no word was spoken, his thoughts came through. He told me with an amused look, "Have you forgotten Jesus turned water into wine at another wedding reception? God is very pleased with what you are doing. Jody is a special child of God. He loves him very deeply. God will smooth your path before you. You are very tired, and you need to rest. Just close your eyes and leave things up to God."

I closed my eyes and relaxed in a deep sleep. When I woke up, I was refreshed.

Saturday night, when I arrived at the church, Laurie was finishing the decorating. Her son, Austin, was setting up tables and chairs. My friends from our church, Loida Virbel, Fay Singh, and Rita Torrez, soon joined me and helped in the kitchen by filling the little dishes with nuts and mints.

Jody's family were delighted to see him after an absence of several years. They stayed from seven p.m. to ten p.m. After the reception, I asked one of the elders of the church, "Where do you keep the vacuum cleaner and mop?"

They smiled and told me, "Don't worry about cleaning up. Just take what belongs to you. We'll clean up tomorrow. This is all part of our Christmas present to you and Jody."

When we packed up to go home, we had six gallons of apple cider left over.

***

Jody came out from Pennsylvania to spend a week's vacation with his family, and the day before he flew home, he came and spent the afternoon with Jack and I. I was so excited seeing him, I am afraid I did most of the talking. He sat with a sweet amused look on his face, and gently teased me, the same way my son, Larry, does.

Jody likes to tell me I was instrumental in his deciding to follow God. This, of course, makes me feel good, knowing this wonderful man of God thinks this way. But the truth is, I feel God led him into my life, to show me that although I am almost ninety, there are still ways I can serve my Lord.

THE END

I was young and now I'm old,
but I have never seen the righteous left all alone,
have never seen their children begging for bread.
They are always gracious and generous.
Their children are a blessing.
Psalm 37:25-26 (CEV)